Walking in Two Worlds

Advance praise for Walking in Two Worlds

"Rabbi Dr. Herbert Cohen has written a unique manuscript, skillfully extending the wisdom of secular literature and bringing it into the tents of Torah. I highly recommend this work to those who live with this vision."
-Rabbi Aaron Rakeffet, Professor of Talmud, Gruss Kollel of Yeshiva University in Israel, author of The Rav: The World of Joseph B. Soloveitchik

"Rabbi Herbert Cohen has created an original and timely work. By amalgamating the worlds of Torah with modern culture, Rabbi Cohen shows how Torah concepts can be found and portrayed even in secular works, while maintaining the primacy of Torah values. Thus, he has demonstrated that the two worlds need not always be in conflict. This work will benefit anyone who wants to explore and find Jewish values in every part of life."
-Rabbi Dr. Nachum Amsel, Director of Educational Projects, Destiny Foundation

"Rabbi Herbert Cohen's masterpiece links cultures with a breathtakingly elegant filigree of formidable scholarship. Walking in Two Worlds is an exhilarating journey with great views en route and a worthy destination."
Rabbi Daniel Lapin, President, American Alliance of Jews and Christians

"Rabbi Herbert Cohen has written a fascinating book on the relationship between Torah and secular studies. While not everyone will agree with his thesis, everyone will agree that his book is worthwhile to read and think about."
Rabbi Michael Broyde, Professor of Law, Emory University, Chaver, Beth Din of America, Founding Rabbi of Young Israel of Toco Hills, Atlanta, Georgia

Walking in Two Worlds

Visioning Torah Concepts through Secular Studies

Herbert J. Cohen

iUniverse, Inc.
New York   Bloomington

Walking in Two Worlds
Visioning Torah Concepts through Secular Studies

iUniverse books may be ordered through booksellers or by contacting:

iUniverse
1663 Liberty Drive
Bloomington, IN 47403
www.iuniverse.com
1-800-Authors (1-800-288-4677)

ISBN: 978-1-4502-3027-8 (sc)
ISBN: 978-1-4502-3028-5 (hc)
ISBN: 978-1-4502-3029-2 (ebk)

Library of Congress Control Number: 2010906631

Printed in the United States of America

iUniverse rev. date: 05/24/2010

Dedications

To Rabbi Cohen-

We have a lot of happy memories of times spent together. You were always there for us and a big help spiritually as well as a friend we could rely on. We are pleased to be able to help spread your thoughts about the interface of Torah and worldly culture.

Dear Friends Who Prefer To Remain Anonymous

In memory of Ronald Gruen, a beloved husband, a Judaic scholar who always appreciated the wonder and beauty of Torah, and a dear friend to many

Ethel Gruen
Dallas, Texas

In loving memory of Melvin Newman

Allison and Phil Cuba
Atlanta, Georgia

Fellowship of Benefactors

In honor of our children, Sammy and Tracey Grant, Andy and Dara Grant, and Jonathan Grant, and our grandchildren, Elizabeth, Jacob, Heather, Matthew, and Sari Grant
Ilene and Adrian Grant, Atlanta, Georgia

Thank you, Rabbi Cohen, for your dedication and teaching excellence.
Dr. George Gottlieb, Atlanta, Georgia

Susan and Paul Fishman, Denver, Colorado

Marsha and Si Londe, Atlanta, Georgia

Joan and Michael Margolies, Dallas, Texas

Egon Petschek, Atlanta, Georgia

Leah and Jay Starkman, Atlanta, Georgia

Sharon and David Westerman, Atlanta, Georgia

In loving memory of Jeanette and Herb Levis
Dr. AnnRita Hader Siegel, Atlanta, Georgia

In loving memory of Harry Umansky, beloved husband, father, grandfather, and great-grandfather. His legacy of gentleness and mentchlichkeit is always with us.

Claire Umansky,Michael and Sherry Umansky and family, Jay and Peggy Umansky and family

In memory of our dear grandfather, Harry Umansky, from his loving grandchildren,

Dani and Diane, Elie and Esty, Rachel and Shia, Ezra, Benyamin and Elizabeth, and Chani and Menachem

Patrons

Jack Bleich

Stewart Bonnett

Selma and Dan Burke

Lucy and Sam Carson

Sheila and Marshall Cohen

Scott Eranger

Faye and Abe Esral

Marilyn and Alan Feingold

Susie and Alan Feinstein

Tracey and David Gavant

Doris and Marty Goldstein

Gladys Hirsch

Sandy and Jack Horowitz

Adina and Jeff Jagoda

Deena Ann Koniver

Ruth and Michael Opatowski

Michelle and Joel Orgel

Marty Orgel

Martha and Jim Reith

Marcia and Michael Schwarz

Marsha and Mark Strazynski

Patrons

Table of Contents

Preface

For the past four years, it has been my privilege and pleasure to work as a Family Educator for the Community Kollel of Dallas. This year one of my special projects was to write *Walking in Two Worlds: Visioning Torah Concepts through Secular Studies*. The project has been a labor of love, for I have spent much of my professional life immersed in that very topic as I served as Principal of Yeshiva High School of Atlanta and yearly taught literature courses to high school students. Finding connections between the Torah and secular worlds was part of the fabric of my instruction. I thank Rabbi Ari Perl, Dean of the Community Kollel of Dallas, and the Kollel Board for giving me the opportunity to work on this long postponed educational endeavor.

I would like to thank a number of people who provided valuable assistance to me.

Thanks to Rabbi Yaakov Tannenbaum, Senior Scholar at the Community Kollel of Dallas, a friend and colleague who read an early draft and gave me many suggestions which helped refine my thinking about the relationship between the Torah and secular worlds.

Thanks to Dan Gail, a good friend, who took out time from his busy schedule to proofread the manuscript and made many valuable typographical corrections and stylistic suggestions.

Thanks to my son, Benyamin Cohen, an expert editor in his own right, who proofread the text with an eye towards making it a worthwhile read for all spiritual seekers regardless of their faith.

Thanks to Rabbis Aaron Rakeffet, Nachum Amsel, Daniel Lapin, and Michael Broyde, who reviewed early versions of the manuscript.

Thanks to my wife Meryl, who reviewed many sections of the manuscript and made valuable suggestions. I often give Meryl my first drafts, and she is quick to spot instances of muddy thinking and gently remind me to clarify ambiguities.

Thanks to the Holy One, Blessed be He, who grants me good health and the strength and focus to labor in the fruitful vineyards of Torah education.

Any shortcomings or mistakes in *Walking in Two Worlds* are my own and should not be attributed to any of the wonderful people who have assisted me.

Herb Cohen
Dallas, Texas
April, 2010

Walking in Two Worlds: Visioning Torah Concepts through Secular Studies

An Epiphany

I began studying Torah in earnest when I entered the Jewish Studies Program at Yeshiva University in 1960. The program was designed for students who had not gone to Jewish day schools either at the elementary or high school levels. In those early years, I heard about the great Torah luminary, Rabbi Joseph Soloveitchik, who was the intellectual force at the university; but it was not until the late 1960s that I went to hear one of his lectures.

I still remember the excitement of the evening. Parking was hard to find on Amsterdam Avenue in the Washington Heights neighborhood of New York. Cars were double-parked on both sides of the street, and people were looking for tickets to enter Lamport Auditorium where the lecture would take place. I arrived relatively early and found a seat in the middle of the room near the left side of the stage. There was a palpable tension in the air; and after five or ten minutes, the Rav, as Rabbi Soloveitchik was referred to, entered. More than 2000 people stood up to give him honor. He stepped up to the stage and sat down behind a table, filled with huge tomes, which served as a base for a microphone. The microphone amplified his voice, but I still had to strain to listen. What I experienced was an intellectual awakening.

The Rav shared Torah insights but in a way that reflected a sophisticated and cosmopolitan understanding of life. He could quote from the Bible and from the philosopher Hegel with equal facility. He spoke for close to three hours, and I was not aware of time as I was mesmerized by his talk. Until now, the two worlds of Torah and secular wisdom were two separate worlds. Now in the Rav's animated lecture, the secular and the sacred merged together as two aspects of one holy creation.

The Rav suggested that all of the laws of the Torah, even the social laws, should be seen as *chukim*, statutes which are not based on reason. There should be no distinction between them and *mishpatim* (rational laws). As an example, the Rav quoted the commandment of "thou shalt not murder." Reason tells us that it is wrong. Everyone will cry if a beautiful young girl is killed; but the Rav queried, what about the murder of an old mean miserly lady, such as Raskolnikov's victim in *Crime and Punishment*? Reason might say that murder is okay in this instance; but if we assume that all laws are simply directives from God to man that should be observed even if they do not make rational sense, then such a crime is wrong. Without such an approach, the whole world will turn into a jungle where each man will rationalize his own behavior

Hearing the Rav was a watershed experience in my life. To my young mind, it represented an ideal synthesis of Torah and worldly learning that became a model for me to emulate. It convinced me that Torah and secular learning do not always have to be in opposition. Clearly, the Rav always functioned on a daily basis with the understanding of the primacy of Torah learning and living and with an understanding that there is an inevitable tension between the Torah and the secular spheres. However, he did feel that there was room for some rapprochement of the two worlds. Indeed, it is the premise of this book that there is much to learn from secular learning if we approach it thoughtfully and critically.

Introduction

For the bulk of my professional career, I have been a Jewish day high school principal, first in Atlanta, and then in Columbus and Denver. Along with my rabbinic ordination, I obtained a PhD in English, inspired by Rabbi Aharon Lichtenstein who was the *Rosh Kollel* (Head of Talmud Studies for advanced rabbinical students) when I was a member of that august group of Kollel Fellows in the late sixties. Rabbi Lichtenstein was and is a master of Torah learning and also received a doctorate in English from Harvard, writing his dissertation on the Cambridge Platonist Henry More. My doctorate was from Georgia State University, where I wrote my thesis on George Herbert, the seventeenth century British poet.

Over the years, I taught literature at the high school level to hundreds of students for two reasons. Firstly, even though I was the head of school, I wanted to have credibility with my teachers; and teaching with them meant that we were working in the same educational vineyard and that I understood their daily challenges. Secondly, I truly felt that I could transmit Torah values very easily through secular literature such as a book or a poem. Even though I was required to prepare the students for standardized examinations, there were many opportunities not only to analyze literary style but also to derive life lessons as well from classic writers who described the agony and ecstasy of the human condition. Moreover, in the secular classroom, it was generally easier to teach because students entered that room more ready to learn and "the readiness is all." In my out-of-New York day school, students, many of whom came from non-observant homes, did not always understand or appreciate the value of Torah learning; and many were there because of parental pressure, not because of a personal desire to study Torah. In the Judaic classroom, there may have been some resistance to learning strange and challenging material; in the secular classroom, there was none.

For close to 30 years, I taught English, American, and World Literature, Jewish History, and film courses as well. During that time, I always searched for points of commonality between Torah subjects and secular studies. Often, they seemed to inform one another. It was a reciprocal relationship, which greatly enhanced our class discussions and convinced me that, even in an Orthodox Jewish day school setting, there could be a degree of rapprochement between the Torah and secular worlds of learning.

Let me begin by sharing certain basic assumptions from which I operated, and then I will share with the reader a sampling of the poems, novels, and films that I used in class to convey valuable Torah perspectives on life.

A Story.

In the mid-1960s, when I was pursuing a master's degree in English at Hunter College, a division of the City University of New York, I took a class in European Literature of the Renaissance. One of the authors we read was the Frenchman Rabelais whose work is filled with profanity. Even though we read the work in translation, the four letter words remained intact. As part of the lesson, the professor, who was probably the best lecturer that I had in graduate school, asked the class to read the narrative aloud. As my turn approached, I felt increasingly uncomfortable. My parents never used profanity at home, I was wearing a *yarmulke* (skullcap), and I did not feel at ease uttering four-letter words, especially in a coed class. When my turn to read aloud came, I simply could not get the words out, and my teacher then moved on to the next student. Although he did not tell me, I sensed he was disappointed in me. He wanted to liberate me from my real-life frame of reference, just as Rabelais wanted to liberate his contemporary Frenchmen from narrow thinking; yet I resisted. I chose to remain in my limited, parochial world.

I realized then and I realize now, as an Orthodox Jew and as a person deeply involved with secular culture, that there is a sharp dissonance between the two worlds. I sometimes feel that the term "Modern Orthodox" is an oxymoron, for to be an Orthodox Jew in the contemporary world may be impossible. After all, the values of the modern world are so often antithetical to the values of Torah. As an Orthodox Jew, I strive for *kedushah* (sanctity) in my daily life, yet the world in which I live and immerse myself pushes me away from it. How should I approach Western culture? Can there be, in fact, a rapprochement between these two opposite forces?

I began to refine my understanding of the problem and develop a coherent approach to the issue after meeting Rabbi Aharon Lichtenstein and attending his Talmud class when I attended Yeshiva University. It was then that I began emotionally and intellectually to integrate the two worlds.

Rabbi Lichtenstein is presently a *Rosh Yeshiva* (dean and chief scholar) at Yeshivat Har Etzion in Israel. When I first met him, he was the *Rosh Kollel* at Yeshiva University and I was a member of that *Kollel*. Moreover, he is the son-in-law of Rabbi Joseph Soloveitchik. For me, he was and is a role model, for he synthesizes excellence in Torah study with excellence in secular studies. Most important, he is a master of good character; and as a person of sterling character he has made the most profound impression on me.

In his lectures at Yeshiva University, he often expressed the view that there is value in secular culture. By culture, he meant the study of the best that has been thought in the world, as Matthew Arnold defined it for his Victorian society. The touchstones of great literature of the past can provide a beacon of light for the future. If properly approached and balanced, general culture can be an ennobling and enriching force for Torah Jews. The best of culture, he maintained, offers us through art profound expressions of the creative spirit, which reflects our being created in God's unique image. Moreover, culture offers us the ability to understand our cosmic context. It can help us cope with the human condition and give us a sense of the moral complexity of life.

When someone asked Rabbi Lichtenstein what he had learned in graduate school, he responded: "I learned the complexity of human experience." He understood that life cannot always be viewed in black and white terms. Grey is the common hue to much of human experience. The great writers of the past enable us "to see life steadily and see life whole." They give us a more comprehensive picture of the human condition.

My assumptions about secular learning emerge from this perspective, articulated over a span of time, in various lectures that I heard from Rabbi Lichtenstein and others. Furthermore, Maimonides informs us in his seminal book *Yesodei HaTorah* (Foundations of Torah) that we apprehend holiness/God not only through Torah but also through God's creations. We learn about God by studying not only His words but also His works. Everything in creation has an infinite potential for good. My task as a teacher of literature is to give students the tools to discriminate between the wheat and chaff of good literature. In the Modern Orthodox schools in which I operated, the assumption was that I could not keep the outside world out, but that I could help students navigate that world from within. Therefore, I spent time in class giving students examples of literature, both contemporary and classic, that made meaningful observations about life that paralleled a Torah world view.

My Thesis and My Method

Having spent the bulk of my life involved in the general studies and the Torah studies departments of Jewish day high schools, I have concluded that the relation between the two is synergistic. Secular studies can illuminate Torah studies and Torah studies can do the same for general studies. Without a doubt, Torah study in a Jewish day high school, and in life, is primary. However, secular studies should not be relegated to the dust bin. There is intrinsic value in much of it, and the argument of this book is that we can sharpen our understanding of both general studies and Torah if we value both as reflections of Divine wisdom. Shakespeare is not to be equated with Torah, but a reading of the bard can enhance our apprehension of human nature and of characters and events in the Torah.

The first section of this book presents examples of the connection between Torah and secular studies as manifested in the weekly Torah portions of Genesis and Exodus. These examples have been utilized in classes I have taught, and I have found that they do indeed sharpen students' understanding of the Biblical narratives.

The second section of the book is geared to anyone involved in a teaching situation, or for that matter anyone interested in seeing connections between Torah and general literature. I present to the reader a number of "teachable moments" that I have experienced over my many years of teaching high school students. My observations are merely intended to show, by contrast or comparison, connections and possibilities for interpretation and for finding meaning in sacred and profane literature. They are not intended as definitive Torah commentary or as literary criticism in a conventional sense. The book essentially is written to open a doorway towards new understandings of both Torah and secular texts.

The third section of the book considers the synergy between Jewish thought/values and contemporary film, which represents another aspect of secular studies. Over the years I have taught courses in film as well as literature, and I have discovered that movies can be influential shapers of lifestyle choices. For this reason, I decided to include a section on cinema.

The more we read great literature, the more we discover how Torah is part of the world's collective unconscious. The great writers of the past understood that the Bible gives us a key to the past and a window into the future, and that is a piece of wisdom worth considering.

One caveat should be kept in mind while reading my book. In the final analysis, the wisdom of the Torah is divine and eternal. The secular works to which I refer do not validate Torah, for Torah needs no external validation. Rather, the secular works that I mention hopefully will illuminate a Torah concept and make Torah more relevant to the serious spiritual seeker. Human in origin, secular wisdom operates on a different plane than Torah which directly emanates from God. It is my hope that *Walking in Two Worlds* will serve as a catalyst to connect people more deeply to the divine messages inherent in Torah text.

In truth, the subject of this book, visioning Torah concepts through secular studies, is vast and deserves much more than my small tome. It is my wish that this volume will stimulate thought about the interface of general and Judaic studies in the classroom and in life; and that I may be privileged, God willing, to expand this work in the years ahead.

Genesis/Bereishit

Bereishit

Hovering Over Us

When educators get together to discuss students and their home environments, they sometimes refer disparagingly to "helicopter moms." The term refers to mothers who cannot separate from the children, especially during their child's early years at school. I recall that in the community in which I served as an elementary day school principal, there was one mother in particular who would come back every day at noon time to check in with her child, bringing him a nicely prepared lunch together with afternoon snacks. She easily could have sent them with her son in the morning; but claiming she forgot, she would always show up at school later in the day to reconnect with her son.

From an educational and parenting perspective, I felt her continual interference in her son's learning program was not helpful; but the Bible gives us another perspective on hovering over something. It is not a hovering over a child, but rather creation itself over which God hovers as He is about to create life. God is hovering over the surface of the waters and He says: "Let there be light."

The great sage Rashi, a medieval commentator on the Bible, remarks that God's throne is standing in the air and hovering over the surface of the water *like a dove that hovers over the nest.* The dove wants both to protect and nourish its young. In some primitive way, it cares for its offspring and wants to give its newborns continued substance and life. It is the motherly instinct.

This kind of hovering is something that God uses to illustrate how we should relate to the natural world around us and how we should treat His creation. Part of our mission as Jews is to imitate the ways of God, and God is showing us how to protect nature and ultimately revere it. We need to hover over it as God did.

Gerald Manley Hopkins in his exquisite poem "God's Grandeur" tells us that "the world is charged with the grandeur of God/It will flame out, like shining from shook foil." The poetic analogy is to gold foil that gives off a shining brightness, which dazzles the viewer when it is shaken. The beauty of nature should dazzle us. Moreover, the poet informs us that, in spite of man's abuse of nature, "nature is never spent/There lives the dearest freshness deep down things." As a result of God's ongoing involvement with nature, it is renewed constantly because God "over the bent/World broods with warm breast and with ah! bright wings." God has created the world and is still nourishing it each and every day. As we say in our daily morning prayers, God "in his goodness renews the world every day."

Reading the Torah portion of Bereishit each year reminds us of the original creation and the creation that is ongoing in our lives. The poetry of nature is constantly renewed because God is still hovering over us.

Noach

The Relationship of Torah to Secular Culture, or the "Good Cover-up"

Although the premise of this book is that there is value in secular culture, this does not mean that it endorses or affirms the value of every piece of literature or art. One must develop the ability to discriminate between the wheat and the chaff of secular learning;

and to recognize, as Matthew Arnold would say, the "touchstones of great literature" of the past so that we can determine the worth of literature that we read today.

For me, the Biblical story that best summarizes the Torah view of the proper relationship between worldly culture and Torah Judaism is that of Noah and his sons after the flood. After the rain, Noah exits the ark and offers sacrifices. He then plants a vineyard, becomes drunk, and reveals his nakedness. Ham sees his father's nakedness in his tent and tells his two brothers who are outside. Shem and Japheth take a garment, place it on Noah's shoulders, covering their father's nakedness while they walk backwards. They do not look at his shame. When Noah awakes and understands what has happened, he curses Ham and gives blessings to Shem and Japheth.

What are the blessings? In this regard, it is instructive to look at an observation that Rashi makes on the text. Although two people *took hold* of Noah-- Shem and Japheth—the singular Hebrew verb form is used. Why? The Midrash, an ancient collection of Biblical interpretations, informs us that only Shem initiated the action of covering his father. Japheth simply agreed with his brother's action; in fact, he was a secondary player. Since Japheth plays a secondary role, he receives a secondary blessing, conditional in a sense. The Midrash tells us that Shem's blessing is to receive a *tallit* (prayer shawl) as a reward and Japheth gets a garment without spiritual significance. Shem's reward of a *tallit* suggests the eternality of a mitzvah; Japheth's reward is a mere garment, suggesting, according to the Midrash, the funeral shrouds of the dead. Japheth's action is a hollow one, without spirituality; therefore, his garment is associated with death.

After this, Noah invokes God's name, telling Japheth that his boundaries will be expanded and that he will reflect beauty, but that he will reside in the tents of Shem.

What is suggested in the Midrash is that there is a unique partnership between Shem and Japheth. Noah tells Japheth that he needs to be in the tent of Shem. He needs the support and direction of the more spiritual and religious Shem, who was purely motivated to help his father and was not doing the good deed of covering him as an afterthought.

Our Sages tell us that Japheth is considered the forefather of Greek culture. Greece is emblematic of physical and intellectual beauty, but without a spiritual context. Greece represents external beauty; therefore, Noah was telling Japheth that beauty/art should be within the spiritual context of Shem.

By extension then, this means that Judaism does not believe in the adage "art for art's sake." Art, rather, has meaning and significance only within the broader context of a Torah worldview. Literature has value, art has value, but only to the extent that they enhance our knowledge and understanding of our spiritual selves. The context is everything.

How does this nuanced approach towards secular culture translate into practical Torah living in the contemporary world? A student once asked me if going to the movies is allowed in Judaism. He knew that none of his Torah teachers had a TV in their homes and that they did not go to the movies, to his knowledge. He, therefore, wanted to know if it was a forbidden activity. I told him no, but not all movies are okay to see. Sometimes movies present to us images of things we ought not to see – immodesty, unethical behaviors, and other unsavory activities. I told him to be guided by the Biblical model.

When dealing with immorality or sexuality in the Torah, the Bible is succinct. The rape of Dinah and the sexual incident of Judah and Tamar are dealt with in a few lines; so too is the story of the concubine of Givah.

What this communicates to us is that we are not to wallow in observing immoral or immodest behavior. We know it exists but we do not want to immerse ourselves in it. Intellectually, we want to have our eyes wide open; practically speaking, we want to have our eyes wide shut. Constant exposure to immorality may taint our souls and make us less sensitive human beings. Constant observation of promiscuous behavior and nudity may make us devalue the opposite sex and perceive them as instruments of physical gratification, not reflections of the Divine image.

Worldly culture certainly has value and can ennoble us, but only if we can discriminate between, as the classic Western movie title says, the "good, the bad, and the ugly" of secular knowledge.

Lech Lecha

The Journey as Self-Actualization

In the beginning of this week's Torah portion, Abraham is commanded to leave his homeland, his relatives, his father's house, and go to the land that God will show him.

This idea of leaving one's home, leaving one's comfortable, familiar environment and charting a new course of life is a ubiquitous characteristic of Jewish tradition. In order to grow spiritually, the Torah suggests we must leave the past behind. We must be willing to inconvenience ourselves if need be, and be willing to uproot ourselves from our own comfort zones.

In truth, the proper state of the Jew is to be moving, not standing still. When we stand still, we atrophy religiously. We need to be dynamic, always evolving, and not be static. Life should be a continual encounter with challenges, which propel us forward towards accomplishment and self-knowledge.

This notion of a journey as a means to self-knowledge comes to mind as we read about Abraham leaving his homeland in search of the Promised Land.

On his journey, Abraham undergoes a series of trials to test his faith. He has to leave his familiar surroundings, he experiences famine, he fights with kings when his family is threatened, and he has to circumcise himself at the age of ninety-nine.

In a wonderful book on literary criticism entitled *How to Read Like a Professor*, author Thomas C. Foster observes that every trip in literature is a quest, and the reason for the quest is almost always self-knowledge. With this insight, I begin to read the narrative of Abraham not only as a holy and seminal account of the origins of Judaism, but also as an archetypal journey of the hero to self-awareness and self-knowledge. Abraham's trials as he travels to the Promised Land change him into a hero for the ages, a timeless seeker of truth who, through adversity, shapes his personality and his destiny.

This image of the journey as a quest for personal awareness can be found throughout literature, perhaps most notably in the classic poem *Sir Gawain and the Green Knight*. Here the poet describes the challenges facing the spiritual seeker, which can be met with an abiding faith in God:

> A hundred cliffs he climbed in foreign countries,
> Far removed from friends, riding as a stranger;
> At every hill or river where the hero passed
> He found—strange to say—some foe before him,
> He met so many marvels in those mountains,
> A tenth would be too tedious to tell......
> Had he not been sturdy and doughty, or served his God,
> He'd doubtless have died or been murdered there many times over......

Moreover, a core concept in this Torah portion of Lech Lecha is that in order to grow one must be willing to change and to take risks. Abraham must leave his homeland, his family and travel a great distance to fulfill his spiritual destiny. He will travel to a land that is yet unidentified in the Bible. And he must do all this when he is seventy-five years old, and viewed by many as an outcast with a strange belief. Yet in spite of all this, Abraham and his wife set out together and begin sharing their new ideas about one God with the men and women they encounter. Their common sense of mission unites them and fortifies them in their journey.

The festival of Sukkot is a holiday of journeys, and the *sukkah* (temporary hut) is a symbol of that journey. The walls of the *sukkah* can be made of stone, of that which does not grow. Its solid walls represent the tangible world in which we live, a world filled with creature comforts. In contrast, the roof must be made of material that is organic, which is now detached from the ground. The roof is made of something that once was growing. It is representative of the spiritual life, of a life that is dynamic, constantly in a state of flux. Dwelling in the *sukkah* with the sky and stars above us is a constant reminder to focus heavenward even when we are surrounded by material benefits and comforts on our life's journey.

The Mishna in *Pirke Avot*, Ethics of the Fathers, informs us that prayer should not be fixed or routine, but rather dynamic and responsive to one's personal situation along life's journey. Like the roof of the *sukkah*, the prayers of the Jew give rise to thoughts of God's protection of us and of our reliance on Him. The fact that prayer is formulaic does not mean it has to be recited by rote, without feeling. On the contrary, it should stimulate us to spiritually grow and be animated by personal feeling, by our idiosyncratic emotional state.

What Abraham's departure and subsequent journey indicates to us, and what dwelling in the *sukkah* with its porous and organic roof indicates to us as well, is that growing spiritually requires a willingness to change one's outer self and inner self, to leave our old baggage at the door.

As we mature spiritually, there is a danger that when we reach a plateau, we may fall into the trap of doing mitzvot in a perfunctory way, motivated more by routine than by a fresh spirit. It is our challenge to keep our spiritual quest vibrant, to regard every day as an opportunity to follow in Abraham's footsteps, and to seek a newer world of spiritual and religious faith.

Vayeira

Extremities

Apocalyptic stories abound in literature and film. These visions of the end of days capture the interest of many who fantasize about the future and who may wonder how they would respond to overwhelming death and suffering that cuts short all of their dreams.

Reading a novel like Nevil Shute's *On the Beach*, which describes the fallout from a nuclear catastrophe, is a sobering and pessimistic experience. Near the end of the narrative, the Australian government provides its citizens with suicide pills so people can avoid the final agony and pain of radiation sickness. It is a dark novel that ends on a note of hopelessness.

When one reads the Torah portion of Vayeira, we see another example of apocalypse, the destruction of the cities of Sodom and Gomorrah. Yet the response to this horrific event is markedly different from the protagonists in *On the Beach*. The daughters of Lot who survive along with their father immediately engage in a discussion of how to perpetuate life beyond the present moment.

What is notable is that they do not give up on life. Their first-hand view of death has not paralyzed them but rather made them committed to finding a way out of their terrible predicament. They understand that extreme circumstances lead to extreme remedies.

Nowhere in the Bible is this strategy more evident than in what the daughters of Lot do after the cities of Sodom and Gomorrah are destroyed. Thinking that they are the only survivors of this cataclysm, they decide to get their father drunk and have intimate relations with him. In their eyes, he is the only man left alive on earth. Their laudable goal: to repopulate the earth.

Subsequently, the two daughters have children from their father. They are Moav and Ben-Ammi, the ancestor of the children of Ammon. What is remarkable here is that Moav goes on to become the ancestor of King David, suggesting that out of sin and despair can emerge redemption and even kingship.

Reading this passage as a teenager, I wondered how it was possible for the daughters to knowingly commit incest. It didn't seem right. As an adult many years later, understanding the context of destruction and despair, especially since the Torah was not yet formally given to the Jews as a nation with its prohibitions against incest, the bold action of Lot's daughters seemed to make practical and emotional sense.

Ben Azzai, a Talmudic sage, in the Ethics of the Fathers, reminds us never to be scornful of any person. This implies that every person has a time in his life when he meets and overcomes seemingly impossible challenges. When faced with such extreme crises, the average man may come up with an extreme solution that in its own unique way may be exactly what is needed.

Chayei Sarah

Looking for Love

The quest to find a wife is a major task of Jewish men. To find one's *bashert*, one's destined one, a person must exert great personal effort and may also need to consult with many friends and relatives, including, of course, one's parents. In the Bible, Abraham is actively engaged in finding a wife for his beloved son Isaac. He charges his trusted servant Eliezer with this responsibility and to travel to Aram-Naharaim, where Abraham's family lived. There Abraham hopes that Eliezer will find a wife for Isaac.

Eliezer journeys there with ten of his master's camels. The great explicator of Biblical text, Rashi, observes that the camels were identifiably those of Abraham because they were muzzled. Abraham's camels would go out muzzled because of his concern for theft. He did not want his animals to graze in the field of others.

Honesty was paramount to Abraham. For such a man, the litmus tests for a suitable wife were truthfulness, sincerity, and kindness, not the possession of wealth.

Eliezer, the trusted servant who came from the home of honest Abraham, determined that the woman who not only gives him water but his camels as well will be the one for Isaac, for she has demonstrated that she cares for all living creatures.

In secular literature, it is hard to find such a concern for ethics and good character when looking for a marriage partner. For example, in Jane Austen's classic novel *Pride and Prejudice*, the parents of Elizabeth Bennett want her to marry a person of means. The key ingredients for marital bliss are wealth and eligibility, not good character. In Henry James' *Washington Square*, Morris Townsend, the suitor of Catherine Sloper, is portrayed as a fortune hunter, interested in Catherine's assets, not her character. In fact, Dr. Austin Sloper, Catherine's father, sees beneath Morris's façade and forbids Catherine to marry him.

One notable exception to this pattern is Edward Rochester's oblique pursuit of Jane Eyre in Charlotte Bronte's famous novel *Jane Eyre*. After ostensibly courting the wealthy and attractive socialite Blanche Ingram, Rochester finally confesses his love for Jane, whom he regards as a pure, simple, and virtuous soul. He tells her: "...to the clear eye and eloquent tongue, to the soul made of fire, and the character that bends but does not break—at once supple and stable, tractable and consistent—I am even tender and true." Clearly, he values substance over form, good character over physical charm and beauty. It is of interest to note that Rochester is many years Jane's senior, a person with much more life experience than Jane. Similarly, Isaac is much older than Rebecca. But the age difference counts for little when the two lovers are on the same spiritual wavelength.

Contrasting such narratives with the story of Isaac's quest highlights the unique approach of Jews to marriage. Wealth and beauty are passing. What remains is good character that lasts for a lifetime.

Toldot

Fasting and Forgiveness

There is an old custom that on the day of a wedding the bride and groom fast. They also recite a special private confession to God and devote themselves to repentance. This custom, according to many Sages, has its origins in the Torah portion of Toldot, which has a reference to the bride that Esau took named Machalat, the daughter of Ishmael. The name Machalat is connected to the Hebrew word *mechilah*, which means forgiveness. The implication is that on the day of the wedding, the sins of the bride and groom are forgiven, for both are newly born spiritually on the day of the wedding.

In what sense was Esau newly born on his wedding day? The Torah tells us that initially Esau married the daughters of Hittites, a nation known for idolatry and immorality; and this caused great pain to his parents, Isaac and Rebecca. Esau eventually recognizes the anguish he has brought upon his parents and resolves to marry within the family, instead of a woman who is a member of an alien and idolatrous nation. Esau takes as a wife Machalat, daughter of Ishmael, an act that, according to many commentators, reflects Esau's desire to turn over a new leaf in his life. Through this match, he has achieved a level of repentance say our Sages.

This notion that the wedding day is a day for confession of sin and personal redemption is the subtext for a crucial scene in Thomas Hardy's classic novel *Tess of the D'Urbervilles*. The two lovers, Angel and Tess, confess their past indiscretions to one another on their wedding day, but with disastrous results. Although Tess forgives Angel for his past debauchery, Angel does not forgive Tess. Their love then unravels with tragic consequences. Hardy describes the scene in heart-rending detail: "He looked upon her as a species of imposter, a guilty woman in the guise of an innocent one. Terror was upon her white face as she saw it; her cheek was flaccid, and her mouth had almost the aspect of a round little hole. The horrible sense of his view of her so deadened her that she staggered...."

In the Jewish view of things, confession is not made to another person. For this reason, the *Amidah*, the paradigmatic Jewish prayer, is recited quietly so that no other person can hear the private/secret failures of another when we beseech God for forgiveness. Jewish confession is a dialogue between oneself and God, and with no other.

Honesty between bride and groom is key, but that should be established prior to arriving at the marriage canopy. The wedding day itself is a day for personal confession to God. It is not a day for reciprocal confessionals. Rather, it is a day for God to forgive man as he becomes a new entity, a new creation, through the wedding ceremony.

Moreover, the concept of forgiveness does not just apply to a wedding day. Rather, forgiveness is a part of marriage as it evolves and grows every day. Marriage creates a reality of shared space. No longer is one focused only on oneself, but one is also focused on one's significant other. It is inevitable that sometimes we say or do things that pain our partner, and that's where forgiveness comes in. Marriage means being forgiving of one another, of understanding that while two people do not always agree with one another, they still need to respect one another and forgive each other. Forgiving in the Jewish view must be proactive and meaningful. To repair a relationship, it is not enough to say "I am sorry." Rather one should engage the other and say, "Will you forgive me?"

Angel does not understand how to forgive Tess until it is too late. In a Jewish marriage, asking forgiveness of a spouse is part of the complex everyday tapestry of married life. We stumble occasionally, and then we forgive one another as we journey through life together.

Vayetze

The Soul in Paraphrase

The seventeenth century poet and clergyman, George Herbert, wrote a passionate poem about prayer. In it he describes prayer as "God's breath in man returning to his birth/The soul in paraphrase, heart in pilgrimage." It is a visceral depiction of man encountering the Divine. For me the poem resonates when I read the story of Jacob's encounter with God in the evening as he dreams about the angels going up and down a ladder. Although the encounter is described as a dream, our Sages view the incident as the occasion when Jacob instituted the evening prayer to augment the prayers of the morning and afternoon, which were founded by Abraham and Isaac, respectively.

Jacob's prayer on that fateful evening is not dry and mechanical. Implicit in the Biblical narrative is the notion that prayer must emanate from the heart and soul as well as from the mind. It is an activity that involves one's total being. In truth, prayer in the Jewish view should not be mechanical. The Ethics of the Fathers reminds us that prayer should be soulful and not recited by rote. Although Jews nowadays have formalized prayer, the Sages who instituted the various prayer services still created opportunities for us to personalize our meditations to God. In my own quiet recitation of the *Amidah*, I regularly add personal entreaties at the end of the meditation before I step back from my personal encounter with God. At that special moment, I always add prayers for my spouse and children, and for success in meeting any specific challenges before me that day.

Jacob wakes from his dream/prayer, and intuitively grasps that God is with him. According to one Midrash, the ladder symbolizes a stairway from earth to heaven. A rung of the ladder represents Mt. Sinai, and the angels going up and down prefigure Moses climbing up and down the mountain. Jacob is given a window into the future of the Jewish nation that both unnerves him and inspires him.

So, too, is it with heartfelt prayer. It unnerves us because we feel vulnerable before an Almighty God; but it also inspires us when we sense that God is with us and that He will help us meet the challenges in front of us. Herbert captures this when he, in a stream of consciousness, catalogs images that confront him while at prayer: "The six daies world-transposing in an houre/ A kind of tune, which all things heare and fear/ Softnesse, and peace, and joy, and love, and blisse/ Exalted Manna, gladnesse of the best/ Heaven in ordinarie, man well drest/ the milkie way, the bird of Paradise/...The land of spices; something understood." It is this kind of raw emotion coupled with deep sensitivity to God's ongoing involvement in our destiny that should animate our daily prayers.

Vayishlach

Looking Backward with Humility

Near the beginning of the Torah portion, as Jacob is preparing for his fateful, tense meeting with his estranged brother Esau, Jacob reveals an essential humility that is a hallmark of his character. He tells God: "I have been diminished/made small by all the kindnesses and all the truth that you have done for your servant , for with my staff I have crossed this Jordan, and now I have become two camps (Genesis 32:11)." Jacob is overwhelmed with God's kindnesses to him and he is now afraid, Rashi tells us. Jacob fears that he has used up his credits with God, and he is again soiled with sin. This makes him vulnerable to Esau's possible attack.

It is of interest to note that George Herbert, a seventeenth century poet and clergyman who became famous posthumously, quoted this verse on his deathbed to his friend Nicholas Ferrar to whom he sent the manuscript of his poetry for possible publication. He told Ferrar that if he thought the poems would help "any dejected poor soul," then make the poetry public. If not, then burn it "for I and it are less than the least of God's mercies."

This sensibility is quintessentially Jewish. The believing Jew does not walk around with a sense of entitlement. His spiritual destiny is directly related to his performance of good deeds, not simply to his being a member of a special people. In the Ethics of the Fathers, we are told that every Jew possesses a share in the world to come, but our Sages warn us that we can lose it if we act improperly. That is why, our Rabbis tell us, the crown of Torah is more valuable than the crown of priesthood and kingship. The crown of Torah can be earned by anyone, whereas the crown of priesthood and kingship are inherited.

At every stage of life, we are challenged. When the Rabbis in the Ethics of the Fathers describe the various plateaus in life at which we arrive (Avot 5:25), the implicit directive to the reader is to consider what we are doing at that time in our lives. How are we spending our time? Are we fulfilling the expectations that God has of us? The Sages remind us that life must be examined periodically, and that the challenges we face at different times in our lives should compel us to rethink life at that moment and make midcourse corrections if needed.

To make adjustments, we need to understand our mission in life. We need to be able to prioritize our future actions based upon an accurate and humble assessment of where we are spiritually and emotionally. When Jacob says that he is undeserving of God's kindness for he has used up his stock of merits with God, he is essentially postulating in all humility that his ultimate fate is in God's hands, not his own. John Milton, the giant of seventeenth century British literature, perhaps best expresses this mode of thinking in his classic sonnet "When I consider How My Light is Spent." Here he states: "God doth not need/Either man's works or his own gifts; who best/ Bear his mild yoke, they serve him best." Our task at various stages of life is to figure out, after assessing our strengths and capabilities, to what we need to devote the bulk of our time and energy. A periodic, humble appraisal of ourselves at that present moment will help us navigate our future.

Vayeshev

True Love

Not long ago I substituted for a teacher on maternity leave for several months at Torah Day School of Dallas, and it was a pleasure to teach Language Arts and History to the 5th, 6th, and 7th-8th grade girls' classes. As I was handing back some test papers, one of the girls noted that I had grey hair, which meant that I was probably older than most of her other teachers. Perhaps I reminded her of the grandfather. Like most young people, she was struck by outward appearances.

In the Torah portion of Vayeshev, Joseph is described by Rashi, the Torah commentator par excellence, as a young man focused on externals. The great sage notes an apparent superfluity in the text. Joseph is referred to as seventeen years old and also described as a *youth*. If he were seventeen years of age, we already know that he is a youth, so why specifically mention this? This is what is bothering Rashi.

To answer the question, Rashi informs us of the traditional notion that Joseph was somewhat self-absorbed. He would spend time fixing his hair and grooming his eyes so that he would look attractive. These are activities of young people who are concerned with external appearances.

Not much has changed in this regard. One just has to look at the advertising in various media to see how much of it is geared towards externals. Appearances are everything.

But this is not the Jewish way to see the world. The Ethics of the Fathers reminds us "not to look at the container but rather at what is in it (Avot 4:27)." Furthermore, the *Eshet Chayil* ode that we sing to the woman of the house on Friday nights states clearly that outward beauty is vain. True beauty is beauty of character, an internal quality. This is a profound message, which finds expression in secular literature as well.

I recently taught a sonnet of Shakespeare, in which the poet declares: "Love is not love which alters when it alteration finds." True love may begin with appearances but it does not end there. People change physically over the years, and love deepens because it expresses itself in ways beyond the physical.

As a younger person, I often wondered when I saw two senior citizens embracing and showing signs of affection to one another how they could maintain their passion for one another over the years. They certainly did not look the same now as when they were first married.

As I have gotten older myself, I now understand that love transcends the physical and becomes deeper through a shared life of joys and challenges that are part of the crucible of life experience. I am convinced that people who are married for a long time feel more love for their life partners now than when they first met. This is the kind of love that Judaism encourages, a love that is not dependent on outward appearance, but rather on shared values and experiences.

Miketz

The Ripple Effect of a Mitzvah

Near the end of Dostoevsky's classic novel *Crime and Punishment*, the author informs us that Raskolnikov, the student who committed a brutal murder, was given a sentence of only eight years in prison. A mitigating factor was evidence that Raskolnikov had supported a sick student for six months while at a university and had gotten the boy's father into a hospital and paid for his funeral expenses when he died. Moreover, Raskolnikov had rescued two children from a house on fire and was burned while doing so. It seems that acts of kindness done long ago changed his destiny.

The story of kindness rewarded many years later is emblematic of a key element of the Joseph narrative in the Bible. In the Torah portion of Vayeshev, we read of Joseph's incarceration in prison and his interactions with the cupbearer and the baker, who were also in confinement with him. Joseph asks them: "Why are you so downcast today?" His question is a telling one. In spite of his own sorry state, he thinks about the well-being of others. He is attuned to the facial expressions of others and to the mood of other human beings. When he sees a person in low spirits, he shows concern and tries to help. Moreover, his question reveals that he has moved from the self-absorption of his youth to a more mature understanding of life.

Flash forward two years later. We are now in the Torah portion of Miketz and learning about Pharaoh's dreams. The cupbearer, who initially forgot the kindness of Joseph, now remembers him and recommends him to Pharaoh, who is in dire need of someone to explain the significance of an unusual dream. Joseph is summoned and he successfully interprets the dream. This leads to his release from prison, his subsequent rise to power and influence in Egypt, and his eventual reunification with his family. All of this happens because Joseph inquired two years earlier about the welfare of another human being. Joseph, in spite of his own personal adversity at that time, was not just concerned about himself and his own needs. He wanted to improve the lot of others.

This narrative is an important one for us and, particularly, for parents and teachers. It reminds us to focus on the welfare of others and not just our own selfish interests. Moreover, it reminds us that one kind or encouraging word can start a chain of events that can influence scores of subsequent generations.

A story: I recently spoke to a teacher in a Jewish day school who told me that, after inadvertently embarrassing a student with an off-hand comment, he went over to the student to apologize. The student, new to a Jewish day school environment, was so taken by the fact that a teacher would come over to him to ask for forgiveness that it made an indelible impression on him for life. From then on, he approached his Judaic studies with more intensity and zeal, for Torah was no longer just another academic discipline to him. Rather, he understood it as an instruction manual for living.

Another story: Recently, a man to whom I had not spoken often came to me after the *mincha* (afternoon service) at synagogue and handed me an envelope with a gift certificate to a local men's haberdashery. I asked him why he was giving it to me and he said that I answered some important questions for him and he wanted to show his appreciation to me. I frankly could not remember the questions, but felt good that our brief interactions were meaningful to him. It was another example of how one small gesture of concern and kindness can be of great significance to another human being, perhaps not immediately but somewhere down the road of life.

All of us, especially parents and teachers, should think of each interaction with another human being, adult or child, as one that may have a ripple effect into the future. Our actions and words are both now and forever.

Vayigash

The Cleansing Effect of Forgiveness

When Joseph finally reveals himself to his brothers, the brothers are nervous. Will their brother punish them for their crime against him? Rashi, the preeminent Torah commentator, in analyzing this touching scene of reconciliation, observes that Joseph instructs his brothers to come close to him because he sees them backing away at this moment of revelation. They are fearful of what Joseph might do. Rashi tells us that Joseph spoke to them at this time using gentle language so that they would feel comfortable in his presence and not agitated. Moreover, when speaking to his brothers. Joseph places the whole story of his descent into Egypt into a Divine context. He encourages the brothers not to be distressed or feel guilty about what happened, for it was the hand of God that orchestrated this entire series of events. God sent Joseph to Egypt as part of a larger plan, leading first to the defining of the Jewish nation in the crucible of Egyptian slavery, and then to becoming a united nation fulfilling a holy mission as they enter a holy land. The brothers were only the instruments that enabled this cosmic drama to unfold.

This ability to see things from the aspect of eternity is characteristic of the committed Jew. He understands that while he possesses free will and the ability to shape his future, in the final analysis, God is in charge of the world and we ultimately are part of His grand divine plan. When events occur to us in our lives, we need to take the long view of things, to understand as best as we can the big picture. The Ethics of the Fathers specifically informs us that the wise man is one who sees the future, who takes into consideration the consequences of one's actions and who attempts to see the Divine hand behind the present stressful moment.

George Herbert captures this multi-faceted view of life in a beautiful poem entitled "Joseph's Coat." Using the Biblical story of Joseph as a metaphor, the poet describes the travails that man endures, only to realize finally that God, in fact, does bring relief to man. The speaker takes the long view of events; hence, man feels a sense of relief knowing that over the course of time one's belief in God makes life meaningful and significant. The speaker rejoices that he now lives to show the Lord's power "who once did bring/My joys to weep, and now my griefs to sing." What begins as tragedy becomes the prelude to redemption.

To move from tragedy to triumph requires the ability to see things from the aspect of eternity. This enables man to forgive, to not hold grudges, to not hate in one's heart. Joseph is the role model for us. His forgiveness of his siblings reminds us to move on in life without carrying the weight of the past sins of others towards us on our shoulders. A dear friend of mine once told me that to live an exemplary life, we must not allow someone else who may have hurt us to live rent free in our heads. When we allow that to happen, we tie ourselves to the past and lose the opportunity to move forward freely into the future.

Vayechi

Passing the Torch

Robert Browning, the famous Victorian poet celebrated for his innovative use of the dramatic monologue, describes a deathbed scene in "The Bishop Orders His Tomb at St. Praxed's Church." The Bishop assembles his close relatives, his nephews, and perhaps his illegitimate sons, around his bed and commands them to build him a magnificent tomb. He is not concerned about his spiritual legacy but rather wants to be remembered for his acquisitions on earth. Moreover, he wants his tomb to be a work of art so beautiful that it surpasses the tomb of any other. He desires precious stones such as lapis lazuli to adorn his final resting place. He calls out: "Did I say basalt for my slab, sons? Black--/ 'Twas ever antique black I meant! How else/ Shall ye contrast my frieze to come beneath?/ The bas-relief in bronze ye promised me/ Some tripod, thyrsus, with a vase or so...." There is no attempt here to understand his children or to give them spiritual guidance, only to convey his wish for an elaborate tomb.

Contrast this to what happens in the Torah portion of Vayechi. Here the sons of Jacob gather around his deathbed to hear some final thoughts of their revered father. They want to hear his wisdom for the ages, and he does not disappoint the attentive listeners.

Jacob is not at all concerned about conveying material gifts to his children. Rather, he spends his final minutes characterizing each son and, by implication, charts a mission for each one of them.

One example of the many lessons and insights he transmits to them is the importance of living together in peace. He wants his sons to understand how important it is for them to relate to one another with love and how important it is for them to support each other, to comprehend that each one's mission may be different and yet still be complementary of one another.

The archetypal example of this symbiotic relationship is the relationship between Jacob's sons, Issachar and Zevulon. Zevulon lives by the seashore, a merchant who supports his brother Issachar who devotes all his energies to the study of Torah. There is no jealousy or competition between the brothers. Each has his own mission and the completion of that mission strengthens the whole. Rashi comments that Issachar "bends his shoulder to bear the yoke of Torah and he became to all his brothers an indentured servant to provide for them decisions on questions of Torah law...and all of their brothers abided by their word." This is the kind of unity that Jacob desired to see in his offspring. It was mutual recognition that each brother was different, with different strengths and weaknesses, and yet all were committed to one goal, the observance of Torah which transcends all individual goals.

What is noteworthy in this scene is that Jacob recognizes that each son is different in temperament and ability, and that his fatherly purpose is to help his children navigate life. To do that, they need to understand themselves and the role of their siblings in achieving their common mission, to serve as a light unto the nations of the world.

Unlike Robert Browning's Bishop, Jacob is not mired in materiality, but focused on the spiritual success of his children. He has much to teach us as parents who want to raise honorable *mentchen*.

Exodus/Shemot

Shmot

Stranger in a Strange Land

Moses is a man of great feeling. Although he grows up in a house of royalty, he does not forget his origins. The Torah tells us that when Moses grew up he went out to his brethren and saw their burdens. He understood that he was part of them and he cared for them.

This notion of caring for those around you, whether you know them intimately or not, is exquisitely expressed in John Donne's *Meditation 17.* Here he writes that "no man is an island, entire of itself/ every man is a piece of the continent, a part of the main.... Any man's death diminishes me, because I am involved in mankind; and therefore never send to know for whom the bell tolls; it tolls for thee." Moses possesses that great heart, a deep empathy for others, and he feels the pain of another.

This awareness of the other is a constant in Moses' life. After he flees from Egypt and settles in Midian, he immortalizes his personal sense of being a stranger, of identifying with the outsider. He calls his son Gershom, which stems from the Hebrew word for *stranger.* The name Gershom is given because Moses sees himself as a "stranger in a strange land," and feels compassion for others who are displaced and vulnerable. Interestingly, Robert Heinlein uses the phrase "stranger in a strange land" as the title of his science fiction novel that describes the plight of Valentine Michael Smith, an earthling born and educated on Mars who yearns for human connection.

The motif of caring for the stranger is ever present in Jewish history. The Egyptian slavery experience forever etched in our souls the notion of sensitivity to one who is less fortunate. We are duty bound to remember how we felt as strangers in Egypt. Therefore, the Torah commands us many times to strengthen the stranger and love him precisely because he is defenseless.

Samson Raphael Hirsch, the noted nineteenth century German Jewish Bible commentator, insightfully observes that Moses uses the past tense in describing his situation in Midian in order not to offend his current family members. He states that he "*was* a stranger in a strange land" rather than I "*am* a stranger in a strange land." Moses does not want to psychologically pain his relatives with a hurtful comment. The sensitivity of Moses moves in two directions, towards family and friends.

Being the outsider is a role the Jew has often played, sometimes to preserve his distinctiveness, and sometimes because the outside world isolates him and compels him to feel alone. This aloneness makes the Jew especially sensitive to others who suffer a similar fate. Moses lived with this total consciousness of the other, an awareness that no man is an island unto himself. The human family is interconnected. Moses teaches us by example to think about the welfare of others, not only of ourselves.

Vaeira

A Snake is Not Just a Snake

The Torah portion of Vaeira has the striking image of Moses' staff turning into a snake. The symbol of the staff and the symbol of the snake are clearly intertwined. The staff represents legitimate authority and enlightened dominion, and the snake symbolizes corruption and evil, suggesting that power--the staff--used incorrectly can corrupt one; or, if used for good purposes, can enhance one's leadership and bring good into the world. In the case of Pharaoh, power corrupts; in the case of Moses, the staff is an instrument that represents the sovereignty and beneficent power of God. Witness Moses raising the staff over the sea, causing it to split and enabling the children of Israel to pass through it onto dry land

We recently analyzed the complex image of the staff in my American Literature class as part of a discussion about symbolism in "Young Goodman Brown," a well-known short story by the celebrated American writer Nathaniel Hawthorne. Hawthorne describes the staff as "snakelike;" and in one frightful scene in the narrative, a traveler throws it down at someone's feet "where, perhaps, it assumed life, being one of the rods which its owner had formerly lent to the Egyptian Magi." Clearly, it is a staff with magical powers, one that evokes Biblical antecedents.

The serpent, who is more cunning than any other beast of the field, first appears in the book of Genesis in the story of Adam and Eve. Rashi informs us that the Hebrew word for cunning, *arum*, also means naked, and it hints at the reason why the serpent engaged Eve in conversation. The Midrash reveals openly that the serpent saw Adam and Eve engaging in sexual relations and the serpent desired her. The snake intended for Adam to eat from the tree. Adam would then die and he, the serpent, would be able to copulate with Eve. The entire encounter between the serpent and Eve was designed to give him sexual access to Eve, to rid himself of Adam as a potential rival for dominion over the world.

Perhaps the most famous literary reference to the snake as an embodiment of deceit and evil occurs in John Milton's magnum opus *Paradise Lost*. Here he refers to the snake as "the infernal serpent; he it was, whose guile/ Stirr'd up envy and revenge, deceiv'd/ The mother of mankind." Shakespeare in *A Midsummer Night's Dream* refers to the shedding of a snake's skin as emblematic of deception.

As Oberon plans to deceive his wife Titania, he observes her sleeping and that "there the snake throws her enamell'd skin/ Weed wide enough to wrap a fairy in/ And with the juice of this I'll streak her eyes/ And make her full of hateful fantasies."

Emily Dickinson expresses her fascination and fear of the snake when she writes:

> Sweet is the swamp with its secrets,
> Until we meet a snake;
> 'Tis then we sigh for the houses,
> And our departure take
>
> At that enthralling gallop
> That only childhood knows.
> A snake is summer's treason,
> And guile is where it goes.

With poets Theodore Roethke and D.H. Lawrence, we see a more ambivalent view of the snake, a view that suggests the erotic temptation that the Midrash attributes to the snake in the Garden of Eden narrative. As Roethke watches the snake of his poem slide away, he tells us: "I felt my slow blood warm/ I longed to be that thing/ The pure, sensuous form/ and I may be, some time."

Lawrence clearly possesses mixed feelings about the snake, and even admires it in some strange way. After observing the snake for a while, he throws a stick at it; but he immediately regrets his action. He reflects: "I thought how paltry, how vulgar, what a mean act/I despised myself and the voices of my accursed human education/ And I thought of the albatross/ And I wished he would come back, my snake/ for he seemed to me again like a king/ Like a king in exile, uncrowned in the underworld/ Now due to be crowned again/ And so I missed my chance with one of the lords/ Of life...." For Lawrence, the snake is a symbol of sexual liberation and prowess; and this is something for man to indulge in, not to avoid out of fear.

An understanding of multiple layers of meaning in the classic Biblical narratives gives us a key to unlock meaning in many works of world literature. Moreover, this adds complexity to our reading and ultimately enriches our understanding of great literature, of the Torah, and of human nature.

Bo

The Significance of Locusts, or a Rationale for Aliyah

I recently had a conversation with a good friend of mine about *aliyah*, moving to Israel. He had been planning it some time and had enrolled with Nefesh BeNefesh, an organization devoted to facilitating the move of Jews from all over the world to the Holy Land. Since he enrolled with Nefesh BeNefesh, he began receiving email from others going on *aliyah*, and observed that most of the emails concerned issues related to young families with children. In fact, there was precious little of interest to him who was making *aliyah* as an empty nester; and he was wondering just a little bit about his planned move. After all, from a convenience perspective, why was he planning *aliyah* when, in fact, he felt very comfortable in America? The question made sense at some level, and then I shared with him my own perspective on this.

Over forty years ago when I was first married, I spent a year studying Torah in Israel. My wife and I developed an attachment to the land, and decided that at some later point in our lives, we would move there. So committed we were to this ultimate goal that we even purchased burial plots in Israel. Life has its own joyful and tragic twists and turns; and twenty years ago my wife died suddenly and I found myself in Israel laying her to rest. Remarried a few years later, my new wife and I still had the dream of ultimately living in Israel.

The idea of living there relates solely to the spiritual advantage of living in the holiest place in the world, where spirituality is palpable.

If we wanted a life based on material things, nothing can beat America; but if we want a life focused around spiritual growth, the best environment to create that possibility is Israel. That is why we still dream of setting up a home there.

The Biblical plague of locusts mentioned in the Torah portion of Bo reminds us of the importance of location. Here Moses stretches out his hand over the land of Egypt, initiating a swarm of locusts to ascend upon the land of Egypt and to consume all the grass of the field. No vegetation remains. On a symbolic level, the green grass represents health, life, and rejuvenation; and Egypt possesses none of these after the plague of locusts. The lack of vegetation is emblematic of the spiritual condition of Egypt. This land, steeped in immorality and self-aggrandizement, suggests Hollywood, a location synonymous with materialism and spiritual emptiness.

Rabbi Adin Steinsaltz in his insightful book *Simple Words: Thinking About What Really Matters in Life* has a chapter entitled "Hollywood." In it he describes Hollywood as a religion that contains the same gods of antiquity: money, power, fertility, and sex. These, to Steinsaltz, "are the abstract gods; their embodiments are the movie stars, who are mythic figures." Hollywood is not a place that fosters a focus on God and Torah, but rather a moral and spiritual wasteland.

This notion finds literary expression in Nathaniel West's famous novel *The Day of the Locust,* which describes the unsatisfying lives of a group of marginal characters in the movie industry in Hollywood. The narrative traces their vacuous lives in a hedonistic society with few moral signposts. Essentially they live in a barren landscape devoid of values; hence the title, *The Day of the Locust*, which functions as a metaphor for a society devoid of morality and meaning.

Images of despair and defeat pervade the story. The people who move to Hollywood are dreamers, who escape daily boredom by reading newspapers and going to movies. They "had come to California to die" spiritually. Tod Hackett, a painter of scenery, is planning to create his own work of art entitled "The Burning of Los Angeles." Faye, a young starlet, is working on a film called "Waterloo," conjuring up images of overwhelming defeat. The final chapter of the book describes a crowd rioting at a movie premiere. Although individuals suffer injuries, the masses can only think of meeting a celebrity entering the theatre. Moral emptiness is the ubiquitous tone of the novel.

Judaism has a different take on life and how it should influence our choice of a place to live, which is discussed in the Ethics of the Fathers (6:9). Here Rabbi Yose ben Kisma encounters a man who offers him great wealth if the rabbi will move to his community. Rabbi Yose's answer is instructive: "Even if you were to give me all the silver and gold, precious stones and pearls in the world, I would live nowhere but in a place of Torah." Our tradition clearly encourages us to live in a locale that fosters spirituality and connection to God.

Rabbi Yose understands that where you live is critical to who you are and who you can become. Therefore, living in the land of Israel is the ideal place to be. The Talmud tells us the "air of the land of Israel makes us wise (Baba Batra 158b)." I suggested to my friend that this means that in Israel we have spiritual clarity and this enables us to be more connected to our spiritual selves and to God as well. When we move to Israel, we are changing our physical homes; but, more important, we are indicating to ourselves that the life of the mind and spirit is more important than the life of our bodies alone.

Beshalach

A Single Man

In my spare time, I serve as a volunteer matchmaker on an international website. I have been involved for a couple of years and have made 2276 matches. However, I have yet to witness one of these couples actually get married. What this experience has shown me is the truth of the Talmudic statement that "it is as difficult for God to match up a man and woman as it was to accomplish the splitting of the Red Sea (Soteh 2b)." I can create the conditions for two people to meet, but I cannot bring them to the proverbial marriage canopy.

The metaphor of splitting the sea with making matches is apt especially today with a very complex and challenging Jewish singles scene. By comparing the amazing miracle of the splitting of the Red Sea, which appears in the Torah portion of Beshalach, to the institution of marriage, the Talmud is suggesting that when two people marry, it is an event that has a supernatural component. The matchmaker may enable two people to meet; but after that moment of introduction, there is an element of the supernatural that must take over.

It is a fact that singles today, especially men, are often confused and unwilling or unable to make long-term commitments, especially when they know that, from a secular cultural perspective, sexual intimacy is not restricted to the bonds of holy matrimony. The average Jewish man, who does not possess an understanding of the holiness of marriage and sexuality, finds little incentive to make a long-term commitment to another person when he can have intimacy without it. And so we have a situation with singles unable to make commitments. Shakespeare in his classic play *A Midsummer Night's Dream* said: "reason and love keep little company now-a-days," suggesting that love overwhelms reason. Today's single men do the opposite. They reason and, therefore, are unwilling to make a commitment to love.

On the one hand, there are some single men on my website who have tried seriously to get married for many years but simply have been unsuccessful. Sometimes a son must care for an ailing or elderly parent, and that has not given him the freedom to pursue marriage.

On the other hand, I know men in their mid-50s who want to marry girls in their 30s, thinking that this is their last opportunity to become a father. They do not understand that girls in their 30s have little interest in men over the age of 50. And so they continue to fantasize about their futures and do not realistically consider simply marrying for companionship and love without children. Like J. Alfred Prufrock in T.S. Eliot's classic poem, they have no sense of urgency in making life decisions. For them there is "time yet for a hundred indecisions/ And for a hundred visions and revisions/ Before the taking of a toast and tea."

The Torah certainly encourages us and even commands us to procreate; but, if that is not possible, it is still a Torah value to be married. The Bible tells us that "it is not good for man to be alone." Aloneness fosters selfishness and self-absorption. Marriage counters that, for it compels one to think about and care about another human being. That concern for the other helps us grow spiritually; and so we continue to make matches into the senior years, for spiritual growth never ends.

Perhaps the role model for single Jewish men should be Nachshon the son of Aminadav, a prince of the tribe of Judah. The Talmud (Soteh 37a) tells us the children of Israel were reluctant to descend into the Red Sea before it parted; and while they argued with one another, one man, Nachshon, jumped forward and marched into the waters. Nachshon was not confused, nor was he reluctant to make a commitment. Ultimately, he made the right decision and, by example, led us all to the Promised Land.

Yitro

The Convert's Less Travelled Road

In my undergraduate years at college, I was introduced to the writings of Bernard Malamud and became enamored with a number of his books, most notably *The Assistant*. The novel tells the tale of a Jewish grocer in the 1950s, who is struggling to make a living in a business environment rapidly changing around him. Into his life walks Frank Alpine, an Italian-American, who becomes his assistant, and who ultimately undergoes a transformative life experience at novel's end. The story concludes with the following lines: "One day in April Frank went to the hospital and had himself circumcised....The pain enraged and inspired him. After Passover, he became a Jew."

The Assistant is a fictionalized story of personal transformation. Frank Alpine, whose very name suggests that he has climbed an emotional mountain, is newly born at the end of the narrative and his destiny will forever be changed.

This transformation echoes the transformation of a major figure in the Torah portion of Yitro. Rashi, citing an ancient tradition, tells us that Yitro was a heathen priest who decided to become a Jew after hearing of the miracle of the sea splitting and the victory over Amalek. Moreover, Yitro, reputed to be a very wise man, explored many faiths before committing himself to monotheism. Hearing of these two miraculous events was only the final impetus for his intellectual and emotional conversion to Judaism. Because of his stature as a spiritual seeker in the ancient world in which he lived, Yitro becomes a role model for converts and becomes one from whom born Jews acquire wisdom.

The Torah informs us, for example, that Yitro gave Moses good advice. He told the great leader to create a judicial system that would work more efficiently for the people. Moses would tire too quickly if everyone waited for him to decide questions of Jewish law. He needed to delegate some of his powers to others and make the lives of fellow Jews more manageable.

Yitro also taught us to use the phrase *Baruch Hashem* (Blessed is God) when people ask us about our welfare. It is a phrase that points to God's constant benevolence towards mankind and the Jewish people in particular. Yitro took nothing for granted and was grateful for the Creator's constant infusion of daily miracles into the world.

Two minor but significant points. Firstly, it is noteworthy that Moses accepted the advice of Yitro. Moses, in this sense, was a paradigm of the good leader. Leadership was not about him; it was about what was best for the people. He was able to accept criticism without becoming defensive and to learn from others regardless of their background or where they were from. This is a hallmark of sound leadership both then and now. In a deeper sense, Moses acquires wisdom from a convert to remind us of the mystical idea that the souls of converts were indeed present at Sinai and, therefore, converts deserve our attention and respect.

Secondly, we should note how deferential Moses was to his father-in-law Yitro. Jewish law places a high value on how we should treat in-laws. They may not be our parents, but *halacha* (Jewish law) mandates great respect for the parents of a spouse. Mother-in-law jokes have no place in Judaism.

The road of a convert is often circuitous. The fictional Frank Alpine depicts one path. Yitro, however, is a Biblical model of the ideal convert, one who intellectually and rigorously examines life, who concludes that Judaism offers a way of life that is thoroughly meaningful, and who commits to aligning his destiny with the destiny of the Jewish people.

Mishpatim

Everything Depends on Justice

Like all good American citizens, at times we are called to serve on juries. I had never served on one before, and so I looked forward to the opportunity to see firsthand how our justice system works when a letter requesting me to serve arrived in the mail. As I watched the lawyers try to determine who would be a suitable juror for the case at hand, I was impressed with their clearly reasoned and articulate arguments, which resonated with me as a Jew. The case under discussion concerned a young teenager who took sexual advantage of a minor, and the attorneys were trying to determine if the jurors felt comfortable rendering a guilty verdict for such a heinous crime when the perpetrator was so young. To my pleasant surprise, the potential jurors spoke honestly about their own biases and some wanted to be excused from serving on such a jury.

Witnessing this entire process gave me a renewed appreciation for the American legal system. It may be flawed, but it possesses a basic integrity, unlike legal systems in other parts of the world. I understood as I observed it why the establishment of a judiciary system is the hallmark of a civilized society.

In truth, the integrity of the judicial system is central to Judaism and is critically important to all just societies, which is why establishing a judicial system is one of the fundamental seven laws of Noah incumbent upon all non-Jews. The Torah portion of Mishpatim speaks directly to this issue when the Torah commands us not to accept a false report and not to follow the majority to do evil (Exodus 23:12). Implicit in these commandments is the existence of a judicial system that is based upon honesty. The Ethics of the Fathers explicitly tells us that *din*(law) and *emet*(truth) are two pillars of the world are (Avot 1:18). Without these two elements, human discourse becomes meaningless, for people can no longer rely on the spoken word. The world is chaotic without the rule of law and assumption of honesty among citizens.

Arthur Miller's contemporary classic *The Crucible* depicts a case where justice is perverted, where judgments are made based on rumor and innuendo, not hard evidence. In this volatile social milieu, people easily lose their good reputations, and even suffer death. *The Crucible* recalls the infamous Salem witch trials of the 1600s, in which innocent people were accused of witchcraft and hung on the gallows. John Proctor, the story's protagonist, is accused of witchcraft by the Salem court; but in a demonstration of personal integrity he submits to death rather than have his good name besmirched with a lie. He cries out: "How may I live without my name? I have given you my soul; leave me my name." It is a supremely touching moment in a play that dramatizes the tragic consequences of judicial corruption. Proctor's cry echoes the sentiments embodied in Proverbs which states that "a good name is to be chosen rather than great riches (22:1)" and Ecclesiastes which states that "a good name is better than precious ointment (7:1)." The Ethics of the Fathers also makes a similar pronouncement: "the crown of a good name excels them all (Avot 4:17)."

The entire Torah portion of Mishpatim, according to our Sages, is the practical actualization of the Ten Commandments given in Yitro, the previous week's portion. A just society cannot exist only by relying on overarching principles; it must transform these lofty statements into everyday justice woven into the tapestry of our daily lives.

Terumah

Loving Work

I once had a conversation with a traveling salesman who was a member of my synagogue when I was a pulpit rabbi. He was commiserating with me about the many challenges I was facing as a young rabbi. He then shared with me his work schedule and I slowly realized that, in many ways, his job was more challenging and tougher than mine. As a traveling salesman, he had to be away from home and family often and had little time for personal growth. His work was tiring and left him exhausted. He was a wonderful provider for his family, but his financial success came at great cost. Although he supported the community by paying large tuition bills at the local day schools, he often was an absentee father and husband. I left the encounter awed by my friend. I was helping the community as a rabbi, but his sacrifices for his family and his financial contributions were no less meaningful or significant to the overall health and well-being of the community.

Our Sages tell us to "love work (Avot 1:10)." Work is intrinsically good, and there are countless examples in the Talmud of great Sages who not only studied Torah but who ran businesses and had the ordinary occupations of manual laborers. For example, the Talmud relates that when Rabbi Judah went to the study hall, he used to take a pitcher on his shoulders, and when Rabbi Simeon went he would carry a basket. Both would say "Great is labor, for it honors the worker (Nedarim 49b)."

Dr. Isaac Unterman in his edition of *Pirke Avot* cites an amazing but down-to-earth insight gleaned from a well-known book of ethical wisdom, *Avot de Rabbi Nathan* (Chapter 11). In it Rabbi Nathan observes that the Jews in the desert did not lead productive lives. Everything was provided for them: manna from heaven, water from stones, and meat from quail. Everybody was a professional; there were no regular laborers. God then tells the Jewish people that every nation should have laborers, and he challenges them: let the Jews make Me a Tabernacle and become laborers, weavers, blacksmiths, and tailors. Then they will be a healthy people and I will dwell among them.

The whole purpose of the building of the tabernacles, according to this view, is for Jews to forge themselves as a nation, to become a productive people developing the tools to set up a vibrant society. So valuable is work that the Talmud states that "whoever works for a living is considered greater than a God-fearing man. Because it is said concerning a God-fearing man that he shall be blessed and happy in the other world. But whoever eats of the fruits of his labor shall be happy and prosperous both in this world and the next (Berachot 8a)."

This positive view of work is championed by the noted philosopher and writer Thomas Carlyle (1795-1881). In his magnum opus *Sartor Resartus*, he speaks of the nobility of labor and the dangers of idleness. To him work is a blessed activity which enables man to overcome despair.

There is a sense of urgency in Carlyle's wish to work and be active: "Whatsoever thy hand findeth to do, do it with thy whole might. Work while it is called Today; for the Night cometh, wherein no man can work (Book 2, Chapter 9)." Working is identified with living a productive life; therefore, we should work as long as we can and with as much intensity as we can.

Our main task on earth is to do God's will, and our priority should be learning Torah. It is clear, however, that we should also be involved and engrossed in ordinary work, for, like Torah, work can be redemptive.

Tetzaveh

A Meditation on Clothes

Recently someone gave me a $50 gift certificate to an exclusive men's clothing store. It was a very sweet but unnecessary gesture; and, in truth, the Talmud advises us to hate gifts, for "he who hates gifts will live (Soteh 47b)." However, I decided to accept the gift and went to the store for a new shirt. What I discovered was there was no $50 shirt or anything for that price, except a pair of socks or a number of handkerchiefs.

As I looked around the shop, I realized that, while I may have preferred a Walmart coupon, there were many people who enjoyed wearing the expensive clothing in which the store specialized. My visit gave me a new perspective on clothing.

Samson Raphael Hirsch, a noted German-Jewish Bible commentator of the nineteenth century, devotes much space in his Torah commentary to clothing, and specifically the significance of the priestly garments, which are described in detail in the Torah portion of Tetzaveh. To Hirsch, clothes in Judaism are a reminder of man's calling. Clothes essentially define a man as human. The special garments of the priest express his unique holiness. The jewels, the exceptional colors, and the intricate weaving patterns are designed to make us revere the priest who wears the clothes as he performs the Divine service. By implication, the ordinary garments of the average man also have significance but in a different way.

Jewish law tells us that clothes should provide protection from the elements, should not be ostentatious or immodest, and should be durable. The Midrash informs us, in fact, that the garments the Jews wore in the wilderness grew with the wearer so that there was no need to seek out new clothes. Our focus in the wilderness was our spiritual growth and maturation, not contemporary fashion.

Thomas More's classic work of the English Renaissance, *Utopia*, presents another view of clothes, which resonates from a Jewish perspective. Here he describes the clothes of the residents of Utopia, an idealized country where the dictates of reason and common sense prevail. People at work in Utopia wear leather garments that last seven years; at home they wear linen or wool garments of only one color so there is no competition in dress. The narrator notes that in other lands one man has many clothes of different colors and materials, but in Utopia there is no interest in such excess.

Rabbi Yitzchok Blau in his useful and highly readable book, *Fresh Fruit and Vintage Wine: The Ethics and Wisdom of the Aggada*, cites a Talmudic source that directly criticizes those scholars in Babylonia who "dress in fine rabbinic garb to cover up their inadequacy as scholars (Shabbat 145b)." In truth, clothes do not make the man, but they do define him in some way. The old adage of dressing for success, understood Jewishly, means opting for simplicity instead of ostentation.

Ki Tisa

The Importance of a Father Figure

Many, many years ago when I was a student in an afternoon Hebrew school, we would misbehave and cause grief to our well-intentioned teachers. I remember vividly that one day when the teacher left the room, we started to have a catch not with a ball, but with a *tefilin* bag with *tefilin* (phylacteries) inside of it that gave the bag weight. Our teacher, who was a Holocaust survivor, suddenly returned and his face turned white when he realized what his charges were doing in his absence. He said nothing. He didn't have to. We were desecrating that which he felt, and what we should have felt, was holy. We immediately sensed the stupidity of what we had done, and the gross insensitivity that we displayed towards someone who had suffered indescribably for simply being a Jew. I recall that event of long ago as I peruse the Torah portion of Ki Tisa, which details the tragic event of the golden calf that occurs when Moses is not present.

The sad and shocking story of the sin of the golden calf provides a vivid example of what happens when there is a lack of visible authority. Without the presence of Moses who is communing with God on the mountain top, the children of Israel become fearful and decide to worship an idol. Although some commentators understand this act not as a rejection of Moses, but as a way to sublimate their worship of God until he returns, nonetheless the worship of the golden calf leaves a perpetual stain on the history of the Jewish people from which it never recovers. The Torah tells us that the Jews not only brought sacrifices to the idol, but they also ate and drank and committed acts of immorality. All of this occurs because Moses, the father figure, is not present.

Lord of the Flies by William Golding is a novel that recounts what happens when a father figure is not present. Ostensibly, it is about a group of boys, survivors of a plane crash, who find themselves isolated on a remote island. At first, it seems idyllic; but without adult supervision, without a symbol of parental authority, the boys descend into savagery, ultimately resulting in anarchy and murder. Good people can sometimes do terrible things when they feel no one is watching and there is no accountability for one's actions.

The Ethics of the Fathers drives home this point where it wisely remarks about the attitude we should have towards our government, which in many ways is our surrogate father, our emblem of authority: "Pray for the welfare of the government, because if people did not fear it, a man would swallow his fellow alive (Avot 3:2)."

At the end *of Lord of the Flies* when adults return to rescue the lost boys, Ralph, the leader of the group, breaks down and cries. Golding writes: "Ralph wept for the end of innocence, the darkness of man's heart...." As we reflect on our own existential states, we always need to remember the importance of the father figure in one's life, who may also serve as a person's Torah teacher and life mentor. Moreover, we need to remember the importance of the symbol of authority, and how it, in a positive sense, shapes the world in which we live.

Vayakhel – Pekude

The Perils of Leadership

When I first served as a Jewish day school principal, I was concerned about doing my best, building a fledgling school, and not making mistakes. Looking back, I realize that my initial focus was narrow. After many years in administration, I realized that leadership is not about me but about students. The question for the day school administrator must always be: what is in the best interest of the students?

This was brought home to me a number of years ago when I had a weak teacher, a father of five children, on my staff. After evaluating this teacher regularly for three years, I concluded that although he was not a strong teacher, he had enough strengths to warrant a contract renewal. During the fourth year of his contract, I believed that things were not getting any better, but I was still reluctant to let him go because releasing him would be financially and emotionally catastrophic for this family.

So I did what I always did when I did not have a clear sense of what to do. I asked a *sheylah* (a question) to an older and wiser mentor of mine. He was unequivocal in his response. He told me to release him. My loyalty, he said, must always be to the welfare of the students, not the teacher. I followed his advice, painful as it was to do.

I learned over the years that leadership always means doing what is best for those whom you are leading. Leadership cannot be about feeding your own ego and your personal hunger for power and control.

George Orwell's *Animal Farm* is a story about leaders and followers. The leaders in this case are Snowball and Napoleon, two young pigs; and when there is a power vacuum in leadership at the farm, they fill it and announce seven commandments of Animalism, the most important of which is "all animals are equal." As the narrative progresses, Napoleon declares himself the absolute ruler, abuses his powers by making life harder for animals, and ultimately creates tragedy and chaos for all.

Originally written as an allegorical mirror of totalitarian governments that took over countries and eventually corrupted the founding ideals of their governments, *Animal Farm* depicts leaders who are only interested in self-preservation and self-aggrandizement. It is an instance of perverse leadership poisoning the body politic.

The Torah embraces a different view of leadership. The Torah's perspective on leadership stresses accountability and responsibility, and being a beacon of inspiration to the people. Leaders should not take advantage of their charges, nor should they abandon the opportunity to be good role models to others. Therefore, to be a good Jewish leader requires selflessness, not selfishness.

This explains why the Torah is critical of the way in which the princes contributed to the Tabernacle. Here in the Torah portion of Vayakhel, the commentators note that the Hebrew word for princes, *nesiim*, has a shortened spelling in this particular instance to indicate that there was something deficient in the way they contributed to the Sanctuary. Instead of contributing first, they waited for the public to contribute and then they would make up what was still needed.

Samson Raphael Hirsh, the celebrated German-Jewish Bible commentator, observes that the princes erred in their calculations. They "had not reckoned on the enthusiasm of the people, so that, in the end, nothing remained for them to contribute except the precious stones for the garments of the High Priest, and the oil and fragrances for the incense and the anointing oil." Moreover, the princes are criticized for giving themselves preferential treatment.

True leaders should be involved with the people whom they lead, should want the best for them, and should lead them from within, not by making pronouncements from above. The princes should have been the first givers, not the last; for leaders are the ultimate lights unto the other nations and the Jewish nation as well.

Teachable Moments

I n this section are references to a variety of literary works, long
and short, old and new, famous and little known. My choice
of works simply reflects what has transpired over my 30-year
teaching career. I have used many different literature anthologies
as well as read both contemporary and classic works; therefore, the
assortment of writers is very diverse. The works cited have at one
time or another been used in a classroom setting to drive student
discussion or to provoke students to think about life in a complex
way. The selections are arranged alphabetically for easy reference.
This is by no means a definitive list. My selections only reflect my
classroom experiences in high school settings, primarily in Atlanta,
Columbus, and Dallas.

A teachable moment: *Aesop's Fables*

Aesop's Fables is a repository of ancient wisdom, and has much to
teach us. In reading some of the fables, we discover many ways to
discuss life wisdom. One particular anecdote concerns the ant and
the grasshopper. The grasshopper is jumping around, mocking the
ant who is slowly and methodically gathering food for winter. The
grasshopper is only concerned about present needs. When winter
comes, the ant has lots of food and survives but the grasshopper
has none. The moral of the story is that it is best to prepare for the
days of necessity.

The fable provides an opportunity to reflect on the story of Joseph, who saves a nation because he requires the Egyptian population to store up food during the years of plenty to sustain themselves during the years of famine.

Another piece of wisdom inherent in animal fables is that we can learn from the animal world. In fact, the Talmud explicitly states: "If the Torah had not been given, we could have learned modesty from the cat (which covers its excrement), not to rob from the ant (an ant does not take from another ant's food), not to engage in adultery from the dove (which is faithful to its mate), and good manners from the rooster, who first courts and then mates (Eruvin 100b)."

The Torah concept that emerges from this discussion is not only that we can learn from the animal world, but that every aspect of creation can teach us something. There is nothing that is superfluous in the world. This notion is explicitly referenced in The Ethics of the Fathers: "There is no item that has not its place/purpose (Avot 4:3)."

A teachable moment: W.H. Auden's *"Musee des Beaux Arts"*

In *Shir Hamaalot*, the psalm that we sing before we say the grace after meals on the Sabbath, King David writes "those who tearfully sow will reap in glad song." The commentators inform us that this is a directive to share the pain of others. That is the Torah way, to empathize and not to distance oneself from those in sorrow. We need to pay attention when our brethren are suffering. The human tendency to look away from the pain of others is captured in W.H. Auden's classic poem. Here he imagines the mind of the Flemish painter who depicts a vast canvas of people not paying any mind to Icarus, a boy falling out of the sky and perishing.

> In Breugel's *Icarus*, for instance: how everything turns away
> Quite leisurely from the disaster; the ploughman may
> Have heard the splash, the forsaken cry,

But for him it was not an important failure; the sun shone
As it had to on the white legs disappearing into the green
Water: and the expensive delicate ship that must have seen
Something amazing, a boy falling out of the sky,
Had somewhere to go and sailed calmly on.

In class the discussion considers our responsibility for others, and paying attention to others. In many places the Torah reminds us to not only be focused on self but on others as well.

A teachable moment: W.H. Auden's "The Unknown Citizen"

In a discussion considering the concept of being created "in the image of God," this poem raises the question of whether we really know a person based upon appearances. In truth, we do not really understand the inner lives of those around us.

The Unknown Citizen
(To JS/07/M/378 This Marble Monument is Erected by the State)

He was found by the Bureau of Statistics to be
One against whom there was no official complaint.
And all reports on his conduct agree
That, in the modern sense of an old-fashioned word, he was a saint,
For in everything he did he served the Greater Community.
Except for the War till the day he retired
He worked in a factory and never got fired
But satisfied his employers, Fudge Motors Inc.
Yet he wasn't a scab or odd in his views
For his Union reports that he paid his dues,
(Our report on his Union shows it was sound)
And our Social Psychology workers found

That he was popular with his mates and liked a drink.
The Press are convinced that he bought a paper every day
And that his reactions to advertisements were normal in every way.

Policies taken out in his name prove that he was fully insured.
And his Health –card shows he was once in the hospital and left it cured.
Both Producers Research and High-Grade Living declare
He was fully sensible to the advantages of the Installment Plan
And he had everything necessary to the Modern Man,
A phonograph, a radio, a car and a frigidaire.
Our researchers into Public Opinion are content
That he held the proper opinions for the time of year;
When there was peace, he was for peace; when there was war, he went.
He was married and added five children to the population,
Which our Eugenist says was the right number for a parent of his generation.
And our teachers report that he never interfered with their education.

Was he free? Was he happy? The question is absurd:
Had anything been wrong, we should certainly have heard.

A teachable moment: Robert Bolt's "A Man for All Seasons"

Here Bolt considers the life of Sir Thomas More, Lord Chancellor of England under Henry VIII. When the king divorces his first wife in order to remarry, More cannot condone his action. Ultimately, he stands for his principles and loses his life. More's decision to remain loyal to God rather than man serves as a catalyst for a consideration of what issues Jews would die for. What are the key values in life for which you would give up your life? This leads to a discussion of the three cardinal sins for which a Jew is required to die rather than commit: idolatry, murder, and sexual immorality.

A teachable moment: Rupert Brooke's "The Soldier"

"The Soldier" emerges out of the poetry of World War I. The sentiments express those of a soldier fighting on a foreign land, while feeling emotionally and physically attached to his homeland. I compare this to our existential connection to Israel no matter where we may be living at the moment. If one were to read this poem outside of the context of military conflict and substitute Israel for

England, one can get a sense of our psychic rootedness to the Holy Land.

If I should die, think only this of me:
That there's some corner of a foreign field
That is forever England. There shall be
In that rich earth a richer dust concealed;

A dust whom England bore, shaped, made aware,
Gave, once, her flowers to love, her ways to roam,
A body of England's breathing English air,
Washed by the rivers, blest by suns of home.

And think, this heart, all evil shed away,
A pulse in the eternal mind, no less,
Gives somewhere back the thoughts by England given:
Her sights and sound; dreams happy as her day;
And laughter, learnt of friends; and gentleness,
In hearts at peace, under an English heaven.

A teachable moment: Elizabeth Barrett Browning's "Sonnets from the Portuguese, Number 43"

One of the most famous love poems of all times indicates that love can be expressed in numerous ways. The simple recital of the words "I love you" are not sufficient to suggest the depths of feeling expressed in this powerful emotion. The poet intimates that the declaration of love from lover to beloved is more meaningful when details are supplied, when there is verbal elaboration. The miracle of love between two people warrants more than one simple statement.

This notion that great events, personal or public, requires expansion/elaboration is manifest in the Ethics of the Fathers which raises the question why the world was created in the book of Genesis with ten statements rather than one. The Sages tell us that this was done to show the great importance of the existence of the world and "to give reward to the righteous who by their deeds sustain the world (Avot 5:1)." The commentators remind us that it is the actions of the righteous who help keep the world alive, and every action of theirs counts and their every good deed is recognized in the heavenly spheres. Therefore, we increase our praise to God for the miracle of creating the world and we take note of the many deeds of the righteous who, together with the Almighty, sustain all of creation.

Love, which provides energy, beauty, and meaning to existence is viewed similarly. It is an emotion that sustains human relationships. It requires constant attention and an abundance of words and descriptions to express the profundity of this transformational human emotion. Observe the richness of Elizabeth Barrett Browning's poem:

How do I love thee? Let me count the ways.
I love thee to the depth and breadth and height
My soul can reach, when feeling out of sight
For the ends of Being and ideal Grace.
I love thee to the level of every day's
Most quiet need, by sun and candlelight.
I love thee freely, as men strive for Right;
I love thee purely, as they turn from Praise.
I love thee with the passion put to use
In my old griefs, and with my childhood's faith.
I love thee with a love I seemed to lose
With my lost saints,--I love thee with the breath,
Smiles, tears, of all my life!—and, if God choose,
I shall love thee better after death.

A teachable moment: Robert Browning's "Rabbi Ben Ezra"

The Ethics of the Fathers speaks of the virtues of old age and the mature mind. The Sages compare the old sage to good wine, aged over many years and sweet to the taste. The theme is echoed in the poem "Rabbi Ben Ezra," which expresses the notion that old age is something to be approached positively. Advanced years give one a rich appreciation and understanding of life, something which is impossible for a young man to possess. The poem encourages man to appreciate the entirety of life.

> Grow old along with me!
> The best is yet to be,
> The last of life, for which the first was made:
> Our times are in His hand
> Who saith "A whole I planned,
> Youth shows but half; trust God: see all nor be afraid!"

A teachable moment: Chaucer's "The Prioress's Tale"

This story of a pious little Christian boy, a widow's son, who is killed by Jews is an example of classic anti-Semitic literature. Emotionally powerful, the reader in a very visceral sense feels compassion for the boy's mother and hatred for the perpetrators of the deed.

The tale provides an opportunity to discuss not only the long history of anti-Semitism, but also the poisonous and powerful nature of slander and how it corrupts the minds of otherwise moral people. Proverbs tells us that "he who utters slander is a fool. In the multitude of words sin is not lacking; but he who restrains his lips is wise (10:18-19)." The Talmud is even more condemning of slander: "Rabbi Sheshet said on the authority of Rabbi Eleazar ben Azariah that whoever relates slander and whoever accepts slander, and whoever gives false testimony against his neighbor deserves to be cast to the dogs (Pesachim 118a)."

A teachable moment: Kate Chopin's "Story of an Hour"

Kate Chopin, an early feminist American writer in the late 1800s, wrote a story about a woman emotionally trapped in a lifeless marriage, but there is a theme central to the narrative that resonates in Judaism: the devastating effects of unsubstantiated rumors.

The story begins as Mrs. Mallard, a woman with a weak heart, is told about the accidental death of her husband Brently. Her initial response is shock and grief, but then she retires to her room in solitude. There she celebrates her freedom after years of marital repression. When she finally regains her composure, she comes down the stairs and at that moment, her husband enters. Louise Mallard cannot stand the sudden change in her fortune and she abruptly dies of a heart attack, or as Kate Chopin expresses it, "of joy that kills."

I use the story as a trigger to the issues of *lashon hara* and *rechilut*, slander and gossip. It can kill reputations and it can cause physical harm as well, creating stress and depression. It is the kind of talk that kills. Together with the students, I explore the *halachic* (Jewish legal) parameters of *lashon hara* and the devastating effects of rumor.

A teachable moment: Joseph Conrad's *Heart of Darkness*

Conrad's novella describes the search for Kurtz, a station manager of a remote African village. Marlowe, the protagonist, ultimately finds him and discovers that Kurtz has taken on the savage ways of the native cannibals around him. He has lost respect for human life and has degenerated into madness. Such are the consequences of leaving society and going off by oneself into remote places.

In the Ethics of the Fathers, Jews are admonished to stay with the community, to share its pain and joy, and to share its common humanity. There is great danger when one separates from the community, and *Heart of Darkness* provides a unique opportunity to consider this seminal Torah value of not separating from the larger community.

A teachable moment: Stephen Crane's "A Man Saw a Ball of Gold"

The notion of being content with one's lot is a hallmark of Jewish values, and it is a notion that finds creative expression in Crane's poem about a man who sees a ball of gold in the sky. Striving for it, he eventually acquires it and realizes it is clay. Yet when he returns his gaze to earth, he discovers that it is a ball of gold, suggesting that wealth lies in front of us if we only we appreciate what we already have.

A man saw a ball of gold in the sky;
He climbed for it,
And eventually he achieved it—
It was clay.

Now this is the strange part:
When the man went to the earth
And looked again,
Lo, there was the ball of gold.
Now this is the strange part:
It was a ball of gold.
Ay, by the heavens, it was a ball of gold.

A teachable moment: Countee Cullen's "Any Human to Another"

Countee Cullen, one of the celebrated African-American poets of the Harlem Renaissance, speaks of sharing one another's troubles in this emotional poem. Every man needs to understand the pain of another, for this feeling connects us to all mankind. This poem parallels the sentiment of King David who speaks of the importance of being with someone when they are suffering: "Those who tearfully plant will reap in glad song (Psalms 126)." The notion here is that when we share the adversity of another human being, we will alleviate that person's pain and pave a way for a time in the future when that suffering will hopefully be over. Listen to the heartfelt words of Countee Cullen.

> The ills I sorrow at
> Not me alone
> Like an arrow,
> Pierce to the marrow.
> Through the fat
> And past the bone.
>
> Your grief and mine
> Must intertwine
> Like sea and river,
> Be fused and mingle,
> Diverse yet single,
> Forever and forever.
>
> Let no man be so proud
> And confident
> To think he is allowed
> A little tent
> Pitched in a meadow
> Of sun and shadow
> All his little own.
>
> Joy may be shy, unique,
> Friendly to a few,
> Sorrow never scorned to speak
> To any who
> Were false or true.
>
> Your every grief
> Like a blade

Shining and unsheathed
Must strike me down.
Of bitter aloes wreathed,
My sorrow must be laid
On your head like a crown.

A teachable moment: ee cummings' "I thank You God for most this amazing"

One of the core Jewish sensibilities is to recognize the hand of God in the natural world. In our prayers, we speak of God who is constantly renewing the work of creation. When a Jew wakes up in the morning, the first words he utters are *Modeh Ani*. "I thank you O living and eternal King, for You have returned my soul within me with compassion, abundant is Your faithfulness." Right before the morning blessings, the Jew recites *Elokai Neshama*. "My God, the soul You placed in me is pure. You created it, You fashioned it, You breathed it into me. You safeguard it within me...."

This sense of excitement and discovery about the natural world is echoed in ee cummings' poem "I thank you God for most this amazing."

I thank You God for most this amazing
Day: for the leaping greenly spirits of trees
And a blue true dream of a sky; and for everything
Which is natural which is infinite which is yes

(I who have died am alive again today,
and this is the sun's birthday; this is the birth
day of life and of love and wings; and of the gay
great happening illimitably earth)

how should tasting touching hearing seeing
breathing any – lifted from the no
of all nothing –human merely being
doubt unimaginable You?

(no the ears of my ears awake and
now the eyes of my eyes are opened)

Compare and contrast this with the translation of the morning supplications of *Modeh Ani* in which we thank God for granting us life after a night of sleep that is analogous to death, and to *Elokai Neshama*, in which we celebrate our being reborn every morning. The poet ee cummings takes the ordinary, represented by his use of the lower case, and elevates it to the sublime expression of God involving Himself in creation at the most basic level. The poem depicts the energy and excitement of everyday miracles. As we say in our daily prayers: "In His goodness He renews daily, perpetually, the work of creation."

A teachable moment: e.e. cummings' "next to of course god america I"

There are many adages in the Ethics of the Fathers pertaining to speech and its opposite, silence. The thrust of most of these aphorisms is that excessive speech is spiritually unhealthy. Scholars, prominent people, are especially enjoined to be careful with their speech, because people will learn from their negative example. In e.e. cummings' poem, the image of a politician mouthing meaningless platitudes underscores the futility of mindless speech.

" next to of course god america I
love you land of the pilgrims' and so forth oh
say can you see by the dawn's early my

country 'tis of centuries come and go
and are no more what of it we should worry
in every language even deafanddumb
thy sons acclaim your glorious name by gory
by jingo by gee by gosh by gum
why talk of beauty what could be more beautiful than these heroic happy dead
who rushed like lions to the roaring slaughter
they did not stop to think they died instead
then shall the voice of liberty be mute?"

He spoke. And drank rapidly a glass of water

A teachable moment: C. Day-Lewis' "The Room"

Reading this poem calls to mind the reluctant leader who finds himself in a position of power, yet who looks to keep himself centered so that he does not believe in what the press writes about him or what the people think of him. In the quiet room of his own mind, he realizes that he is a mere mortal, not a god worthy of people's devotion.

The Ethics of the Fathers instructs us to "despise lordliness and do not become familiar with the government (Avot 1:10)." The implication of this maxim is that the closer we are to the corridors of power, the less we are in touch with ourselves and our good instincts. Therefore, we need always to remind ourselves of who we really are. "The Room" suggests an imaginary scene of someone in power who wants an opportunity to see himself as he truly is, not as others see him.

I use this poem to convey a sense of the solitude felt by Joseph in the Egyptian palace, and to discuss the importance of staying focused on reality when your position in society allows you to create your own reality independent of who you really are.

To this room—it was somewhere at the palace's
Heart, but no one, not even visiting royalty
Or reigning mistress, ever had been inside it—
To this room he'd retire.
Graciously giving himself to, guarding himself from
Courtier, suppliant, stiff ambassador,
Supple assassin, into this unviewed room
He, with the air of one urgently called from
High affairs to some yet loftier duty,
Dismissing them all, withdrew.

And we imagined it suitably fitted out
For communing with a God, for meditation
On the Just City....He
Alone could know the room as windowless
Though airy, bare yet filled with the junk you find
In any child-loved attic; and how he went there
Simply to taste himself, to be reassured
That under the royal action and abstraction
He lived in, he was real.

A teachable moment: Emily Dickinson's "Faith is a Fine Invention"

The image of Jacob's ladder is a seminal one in Jewish tradition. Many rabbinic sages explain it as a metaphor of the Jewish approach to miracles as well as the Jewish approach to life itself. The ladder has its feet on the ground yet it soars heavenward. This tells us that while we should aspire to spirituality and holiness, we still need to keep our feet on the ground. Moreover, we cannot and ought not rely on miracles. Rather, we should do whatever we can in the real world to ensure our success in any endeavor. This ambivalent response to miracles/faith is captured in Emily Dickinson's brief poem, which I sometimes use at the beginning of the class as a motivating device when we discuss Jacob's ladder.

Faith is a fine invention
When gentlemen can see,
But microscopes are prudent
In an emergency.

A teachable moment: Emily Dickinson's "Tell All the Truth"

It is a well-known passage in the Talmud that discusses when it is legitimate to veer from telling the truth. For example, in praising the homely bride, the House of Hillel tells us to say how beautiful she is even if she is not (Ketubot 17a). The thrust of this directive is to encourage the groom to value his new life partner once the marriage has taken place.

Moreover, Jewish law informs us that there are times when telling the truth can hasten death, such as when we inform an ill person that he has a terminal illness. In such a case, it is incumbent upon us to weigh carefully the impact of our words, and at times either not utter them or say them in a gradual way so that the listener can thoughtfully and constructively manage negative news. It is this to which the Dickinson poem refers. Telling the absolute truth at all times is not absolutely required.

Tell all the truth but tell it slant,
Success in circuit lies,
Too bright for our infirm delight
The truth's superb surprise;

As lightning to the children eased
With explanation kind,
The truth must dazzle gradually
Or every man be blind.

A teachable moment: John Donne's "Holy Sonnet 10"

John Donne's famous sonnet, whose opening lines became the title of John Gunther's book about his cancer-afflicted son, speaks of the impotency of death as an all powerful force. Although death strikes fear in the hearts of men, Donne, a cleric, views this life not as the final end. After death, there is life in the world-to-come, in which death has no dominion.

The poem reflects Judaism's belief in the afterlife and echoes Isaiah who says that God "will eliminate death forever and the Lord God will wipe tears from all faces (25:8)." Death, in the final analysis, does not rule; rather God does. The poem serves to stimulate discussion about ultimate values, and about confronting the fear of death. Perhaps one facing terminal illness or death can find some comfort in Donne's words.

Death be not proud, though some have called thee
Mighty and dreadful, for thou art not so;
For those whom thou think'st thou doest overthrow
Die not, poor Death, nor yet canst thou kill me.
From rest and sleep, which but thy pictures be,
Much pleasure; then from thee much more must flow,
And soonest our best men with thee do go.
Rest of their bones, and soul's delivery.
Thou art slave to fate, chance, kings, and desperate men,
And dost with poison, war, and sickness, dwell,
And poppy or charms can make us sleep as well
And better than thy stroke; why swell'st thou then?
One short sleep past, we wake eternally
And death shall be no more; Death, thou shalt die.

A teachable moment: John Donne's "Meditation 17"

Another work often used in my class is John Donne's "Meditation 17," in which he reflects on the meaning of life from the vantage point of one undergoing a life-threatening illness. Donne, an Anglican priest, exhibits a transcendent concern for others at this time and is concerned not only about his own health. Rather, he sees his illness in a cosmic context, and the experience makes him more sensitive to others. Note the following lines, which have become immortalized in books and speeches throughout the years.

> all mankind is of one author and is one volume; when one man dies, one chapter is not torn out of the book, but translated into a better language; and every chapter must be so translated. God employs several translators; some pieces are translated by age, some by sickness, some by war, some by justice; but God's hand is in every translation, and his hand shall bind up all our scattered leaves again for that library where every book shall lie open to one another. As therefore the bell that rings to a sermon calls not upon the preacher only, but upon the congregation to come, so this bell calls us all; but how much more me, who am brought so near the door by this sickness.

> No man is an island, entire of itself; every man is a piece of the continent, a part of the main. If a clod be washed away by the sea, Europe is the less, as well as if a promontory were, as well as if manor of thy friend's or of thine own were. Any man's death diminishes me because I am involved in mankind, and therefore never send to knows for whom the bell tolls; it tolls for thee...

Several Torah values emerge from the above lines. Firstly, since everybody in the world comes from Adam, we are all connected. When someone dies, we feel the loss at some level, for we are one human family. Moreover, as Jews we believe that God's hand is always operative in everything that happens. People may die in different circumstances, but God's involvement in the destiny of all men is part of the Jewish view of life. When I read this meditation in class, I share with my students the eye-opening experience that I had when, as a young Jewish day school student, I accompanied a teacher of mine on his way to make a solicitation on behalf of our school. As we walked the streets of Far Rockaway, we passed a newsstand with papers emblazoned with headlines about a terrible plane crash that claimed over a hundred lives. My teacher stopped and tears welled up in his eyes. He felt at one with all of mankind; and the loss of life, even though he knew no one who perished, affected him deeply. The loss of human life touched him in a personal way, and that is a Torah sensibility: to feel the pain of others.

Furthermore, the Talmud tells us that it is better to visit a house of mourning than a house of feasting (Ketubot 72a). The commentators tell us that there is much to be learned from such a visit, for it implicitly confronts us with our own mortality, and makes us conscious of the value of time. In this sense, Donne's meditation on death causes us to value other human beings and to value each and every day of life.

A teachable moment: Fyodor Dostoevsky's *Crime and Punishment*

The protagonist of the novel, Raskolnikov, is a poor student, unable to pay his rent and to buy food. He is a desperate man, without friends, and his desperate remedy is to rob and murder an elderly pawnbroker. He justifies the robbery and murder by rationalizing that he will now be able to save his sister from a bad marriage and his mother from extreme poverty.

Two topics for discussion emerge. First, there is the question of rationalization for an immoral act. Judaism stresses accountability to God for one's deeds. No amount of rationalization can justify murder. Second, there is the Torah imperative to strengthen our brother if he becomes impoverished (Leviticus 25:25). The wording in the Torah implies that a person does not become poverty-stricken in a day. It is a process that occurs gradually, and we need to intervene before he fails totally. Also note the language in the Torah regarding the fellow Jew who becomes impoverished. He is referred to as "your brother." We have to perceive others in distress as our brothers, and extend them a helping hand before they reach bottom.

Raskolnikov's problem in *Crime and Punishment* is magnified because he is alone. His isolation creates an environment for him to reach for extreme solutions, for he has no one to whom to look for guidance and friendship, to assist him in placing his poverty into perspective and to give him encouragement. The message here is to be proactive in connecting to those less fortunate than we, and to extend to them financial and emotional aid as soon as possible. After all, we are all family.

A teachable moment: Henry Dumas' "Thought"

Although very short in length, the poet expresses a profound truth in life about hate, which stimulates me to ask the class to consider the power of spreading love in the world around us. Consider for a moment the poem's direct and insightful message:

Hate is also creative:
It creates more hate.

The Torah commands us not to hate: "You shall not hate your brother in your heart (Leviticus 19:17)." Hatred is an emotion that is all-consuming, and allows other people to live rent free in one's head. It perverts good judgment and fosters bad decision-making. The Talmud states that baseless hatred caused the destruction of the Second Temple; the story of the ill will between Kamtza and Bar Kamtza illustrates the evils of hatred which exists between two people, and then infects the entire nation (Gittin 55b). Moreover, the Talmud explicitly states in the name of Rabbi Nehemiah the terrible punishment for causeless hatred: "as punishment for causeless hate, strife multiplies in a man's house, his wife miscarries, and his sons and daughters die young (Shabbat 32b)." Because it is in the nature of hatred to grow and fester, it is so important to stress its opposite, love of one's fellow man, at every opportunity to create a healthy society.

A teachable moment: Robert Frost's "Mending Wall"

In his poem "Mending Wall," Robert Frost concludes with the oft-quoted phrase "Good fences make good neighbors." It is a classic line filled with poetically charged language. Like all good poems, it is open to multiple interpretations. As I read the poem recently, I realized that it is a meditation on human relationships: how much do we open ourselves to others and how much do we restrict entry to others. The poem is about balance in human relationships, between respect for privacy and being willing to engage the greater world around us.

This notion of balance resonates in the *halachot* (Jewish laws) pertaining to the roof and walls of the *sukkah*. The roof consists of material of vegetable origin and must shade the majority of the *sukkah*, but it should not be so dense as to provide absolute shelter from rain. Moreover, the walls should not be higher than 20 *amot* (approximately 40 feet) and not less that 10 *tefachim* (approximately three feet). One of the commentators notes that when walls are very high, they separate people. If they are too low, then anyone can come in. There is no privacy. The Talmud relates this concept to school admissions. When the standards are very high, only the elite can enter and many students who potentially can grow from being in such a school may never be able to enter. Conversely, if the barriers to admission are too low, then standards may very well go down.

This notion applies to our personal relationships as well. A person can create barriers between himself and others by being unfriendly or inconsiderate. On the other hand, if a person does not erect any walls between himself and others, he can become meddlesome and interfere in the affairs of others. He will not respect their privacy.

The ideal, Jewish tradition suggests, is to follow the golden mean, and maintain balance between the two extreme positions. It is proper that we are concerned about personal privacy, but this does not mean we should sacrifice our concern for others. The laws pertaining to the walls of a *sukkah* present only one example of where a Torah value and a secular source can illuminate one another.

A teachable moment: Robert Frost's "The Road Not Taken"

Abraham, the founder of monotheism, followed the beat of a different drummer. He is known as *Avraham ha-Ivri*, the man who lived on the other side of the river. Abraham did not follow the crowd. That is his living legacy. He reminds us that it is okay to be different, to choose the difficult path if that is the one leading to God. The Jews have always been a people apart, ready to forge their own unique destiny rather than adopt the prevailing faith. This readiness to be different and to travel a solitary path is the way of Abraham and the way of Jews throughout the ages. This singular resolve to go our own way is expressed in lines from Frost's perhaps most oft-quoted poem, which I have used at times to introduce the story of Abraham leaving his birthplace and journeying to an unknown land.

Two roads diverged in a wood. And I—
I took the one less traveled by,
And that has made all the difference.

A teachable moment: Robert Frost's "Stopping by Woods on a Snowy Evening"

It is a Torah value to maximize one's potential, to make use of every available moment that God gives us. In describing the patriarch Abraham, the Torah tells us that he was "coming in years." Most commentators understand the unusual phrase to mean that Abraham, even as an old man, did not slow down. He made each day count. He never looked forward to retirement and desired to make his life relevant as long as he had the strength. This is the theme of Frost's poem, which ends with the quintessential line "And I have miles to go before I sleep." Even in the dead of winter, which is emblematic of death, the speaker reminds himself that he still has much to accomplish and that he will not retire until God retires him.

Whose woods these are I think I know.
His house is in the village though;
He will not see me stopping here
To watch his woods fill up with snow.

My little horse must think it queer
To stop without a farmhouse near
Between the woods and frozen lake
The darkest evening of the year.

He gives his harness bells a shake
To ask if there is some mistake.
The only other sound's the sweep
Of easy wind and downy flake.

The woods are lovely dark and deep.
But I have promises to keep,
And miles to go before I sleep,
And miles to go before I sleep.

A teachable moment: Oliver Goldsmith's *The Vicar of Wakefield*

Goldsmith's story provides two valuable points of discussion. First, it is patterned after the book of Job, in which a basically good man undergoes a supreme test of faith. He loses everything, yet he persists in his belief in Divine Providence. Ultimately he is rewarded for having endured the trial. So too is it with the vicar Dr. Primrose, his wife, and his family of six children. He loses his savings to an investor who absconds with his money on the evening of his son George's wedding. The wedding is called off by the bride's family. Later in the narrative, Primrose's house is destroyed in a fire and he goes to jail for not paying his rent. More bad news follows; and then, suddenly, there is a reversal of almost all the tragic events and everything ends on a note of joy. Dr. Primrose's wealth is restored and his children marry happily.

A constant throughout all this family turmoil is the consistent optimism and faith of Dr. Primrose, who believes in a God who eventually rights all wrongs, if not in this world then in the next. Contrasting philosophy to religion, he says that

> religion comforts on a higher strain. Man is here, it tells us, fitting up his mind, and preparing it for another abode. When a good man leaves the body, and all is a glorious mind, he will find that he has been making himself a heaven of happiness here; while the wretch that has been maimed and contaminated by his vices, shrinks from his body in terror, and finds that he has anticipated the vengeance of Heaven. To religion, then, we must hold, in every circumstance of life, for our truest comfort: for if already we are happy, it is a pleasure to think that we can make that happiness unending; and if we are miserable, it is very consoling to think there is a place of rest. Thus, to the fortunate, religion holds out a continuance of bliss; to the wretched, a change from pain.

Dr. Primrose believes in a just God overseeing a world in which good and evil get their just desserts. He does not pretend to know why things happen; but he is quietly confident that, from the aspect of eternity, life has meaning, and this is a very Jewish perspective on life.

Second, what transpires at the end of *The Vicar of Wakefield* very much echoes the Purim story in the Book of Esther, in which all the bad is reversed suddenly with King Achashverosh's discovery of Haman's treachery. The Purim *Megillah* (Scroll of Esther) tells us that "on the day that the enemies of the Jews hoped to have power over them, things were turned around and the Jews had rule over those who hated them (Esther 9:1)." The message here is the old adage: "It's not over till it's over." Or as one of my teachers used to say about a closely contested football contest: "The two-minute warning can be an eternity."

What our Sages have said to us and what Goldsmith says through his characters is that we should never despair. God is in charge of the world and salvation may yet come.

A teachable moment: Thomas Gray's "Elegy Written in a Country Churchyard"

The Ethics of the Fathers warns us not to seek glory and to avoid mingling with people in positions of power. Ultimately, such pursuits will not lead to lasting benefits or lasting relationships. The futility of seeking glory is brought home in the memorable lines in Gray's elegy, a key phrase of which was used as the title to a powerful ant-war film by Stanley Kubrick.

The boast of heraldry, the pomp of power,
And all that beauty, all that wealth e'er gave,
Awaits alike the inevitable hour
The paths of glory lead but to the grave.

A teachable moment: Thomas Hardy's "The Convergence of the Twain"

Hardy is not a religious man, but his poem touches on important themes that run through Torah literature. One is the theme of vanity. King Solomon reminds us that material wealth, a concern for the acquisition of things, is a pointless pursuit in the final analysis. The only thing we take with us to grave is our good deeds. Moreover, the poem emphasizes that man is not fully in control of his destiny. We can only control input; the outcome is in God's hands, or, in Hardy's view, in the hands of fate. Certain uncertainty is a reality that all men must face whether or not they are people of faith. The poem, serving as a meditation on the tragedy of the sinking of the Titanic, is useful as a trigger for a discussion about man's inability to control events in life. Man is not in charge of everything that happens to him, even though he possesses the technological ingenuity to bring about great scientific advances.

I
In a solitude of the sea
Deep from human vanity,
And the Pride of Life that planned her, stilly couches she.

II
Steel chambers, late the pyres
Of her salamandrine fires,
Cold currents thrid, and turn to rhythmic tidal lyres.

III
Over the mirrors meant
To glass the opulent
The sea-worms crawls—grotesque, slimed, dumb, indifferent.

IV

Jewels in joy designed

To ravish the sensuous mind

Lie lightless, all their sparkles bleared and black and blind.

V

Dim moon-eyed fishes near

Gaze at the gilded gear

And query: "What does this vaingloriousness down here?"...

VI

Well: while was fashioning

This creature of cleaving wing,

The Immanent Will that stirs and urges everything

VII

Prepared a sinister fate

For her—so gaily great—

A Shape of Ice, for the time far and dissociate.

VIII

And as the smart ship grew

In stature, grace, and hue,

In shadowy silent distance grew the Iceberg too.

IX

Alien they seemed to be:

No mortal eye could see

The intimate welding of their later history.

X

Or sign that they were bent

By paths coincident

On being anon twin halves of one august event,

XI

Till the Spinner of Years

Said "Now!" And each one hears,

And consummation comes, and jars two hemispheres.

A teachable moment: Nathaniel Hawthorne's *The Scarlet Letter*

The Scarlet Letter offers much in the way of illuminating Torah concepts. Let us begin with the names of some of the major characters. There is Arthur Dimmesdale, Roger Chillingworth, and the child Pearl. The names suggest the character of each person. Dimmesdale is in moral darkness, psychologically tormented and confused by his transgression and unable to set things right. Chillingworth is cold, an unfeeling man who does not hesitate to ruin the reputation of another human being. Pearl is the innocent child, pure as the whitest pearl and untainted by the sin of her parents.

In Judaism, names also have significance and often give us insights into people. This is why naming a child is such a momentous occasion, and it is done in the synagogue when the Torah is being read or at the circumcision ceremony. The name identifies the distinguishing characteristic of the person, and often points to the destiny of that individual. This same reason is the basis for the custom of inserting a passage that alludes to one's Hebrew name at the end of the silent meditation, which is recited by observant Jews three times a day.

Dimmesdale commits adultery and suffers unending remorse. The process of repentance is the subtext for one of America's great novels. In Judaism, repentance requires recognition of the sin, resolving not to do it again, and making an oral confession to oneself. Dimmesdale does this and so expiates his sin in the process. These various stages of repentance and their emotional and psychological aftereffects can be seen in *The Scarlet Letter*.

A teachable moment: Nathaniel Hawthorne's "Young Goodman Brown"

Young Goodman Brown embarks on a dangerous journey as the story opens. He leaves his wife, aptly named Faith, to travel through a dark forest to meet the devil. On the way he encounters hypocritical clergymen and various representations of evil. It is a classic story of good versus evil, which provides the context for a parallel discussion of the battle between the *yetzer tov* (man's good inclination) and the *yetzer hara* (man's evil inclination) Moreover, there is much Biblical imagery in the story, which can add another layer of classroom discussion synthesizing Judaic and secular knowledge. For example, a dominant symbol in the story is a staff, but this one is not used by a redeemer like Moses. Rather, it is associated with the devil and the world of the Egyptian magicians. In fact, the staff is described as bearing "the likeness of a great black snake."

Once Young Goodman Brown forsakes faith, he loses his way spiritually. One mistake leads to another until he becomes a man devoid of spirituality and vitality. Echoes of the Ethics of the Fathers appear in the narrative. As the Rabbis tell us, "One sin leads to another (Avot 4:2)." An analysis of Hawthorne's story provides the reader with a visual representation of the Torah/Talmudic notion that sin leads man to lose his moral focus, and the commission of one sin leads to another.

A teachable moment: Robert Hayden's "Those Winter Sundays"

Hayden's poem provides the occasion for a consideration of the *mitzvah* (commandment) of honoring parents. He quietly describes how his father rose on cold mornings to heat the house. The children are unaware of his daily efforts to provide his family with a home that was warm and loving both in a physical and emotional sense. The *Sefer HaChinuch*, a book listing the reasons for all the commandments, notes that the essential reason for this *mitzvah* is to express gratitude to our parents for both bringing us into the world and doing so much for us during the entire course of our lives. The poem highlights the things that parents do that are often unnoticed, but which still should be recognized by their children.

> Sundays too my father got up early
> and put his clothes on in the blueback cold,
> then with cracked hands that ached
> from labor in the weekday weather made
> banked fires blaze. No one ever thanked him.
> I'd wake and hear the cold splintering, breaking,
> When the rooms were warm, he'd call,
> and slowly I would rise and dress,
> fearing the chronic angers of that house,
>
> Speaking indifferently to him
> who had driven out the cold
> and polished my good shoes as well.
> What did I know, what did I know
> of love's austere and lonely offices?

A teachable moment: George Herbert's "Aaron"

When we read about the garments of the priests in the Bible, we implicitly learn about the significance of clothes. Each and every article of the priest's dress is significant and has meaning. Each garment sends a message both to the wearer of the garment and the one who observes the priest in the garment. There is meaning in what we wear.

Compare this to a poem by the seventeenth century British poet George Herbert, entitled "Aaron," in which he describes the priest's garb. Herbert, a Christian clergyman, understood that the clothes of the priest were designed with a moral purpose, and that the priest is representative of all men. Therefore, clothes are not neutral. Rather they are carriers of meaning. This is probably why Chassidim wear special garb and why so many Orthodox Jews wear black hats. It is a silent statement of who they are and where they are Jewishly. What we wear influences our spirituality.

A teachable moment: George Herbert's "Easter Wings"

Jews pray three times a day, in the morning, afternoon, and evening. The patriarch Jacob instituted the evening prayer. His prayer is a plea for safe haven during a lonely and threatening night, in a nameless location on the road traveling to an unknown future. He led the existence of the *galut* Jew, the Jew in exile, moving from place to place and dealing with a conniving world. Yet he triumphs over adversity, for adversity has taught him to be strong in the face of the enemy.

Compare Jacob's spiritual journey with the movement of the persona in George Herbert's "Easter Wings." Although his poem emerges from a Christian worldview, the spiritual journey described in the poem can relate to the journey of any man of faith. It is a movement from light to darkness and then a return to light. The signature lines in the poem that express this religious voyage are "Then shall the fall further the flight in me" and "Affliction shall advance the flight in me." These lines reflect a Torah sensibility. In the Jewish view, the use of adversity is to bring man close to the Creator.

A teachable moment: Robert Herrick's "To the Virgins, to Make Much of Time"

The value of time is a quintessential Torah value. The Ethics of the Fathers states "If not now, when (Avot 1:14)?" The Torah Jew is to master the moment, to make each minute of each day count.

Although one can perform God's commandments even until and through old age, the best time to master time is in one's youth. Marriage, in particular, is a commandment that should be fulfilled as soon as possible. Jewish law and practice encourages marriage from age eighteen and onward, and to postpone marriage is viewed negatively in Judaism. Herrick's poem expresses this *carpe diem/seize the day* notion in secular terms, but the poem's essential point about not squandering one's youth transcends the secular context and can relate to a Torah perspective on life as well.

Gather ye rosebuds while ye may
Old Time is still a-flying;
And this same flower that smiles today
Tomorrow will be dying.

The glorious lamp of heaven, the Sun,
The higher he's a-getting;
The sooner will his race be run,
And nearer he's to setting.

That age is best which is the first,
When youth and blood are warmer;
But being spent, the worse, and worst
Times, still succeed the former.

Then be not coy, but use your time;
And while ye may, go marry;
For having lost but once your prime,
You may for ever tarry.

A teachable moment: Washington Irving's *Rip Van Winkle*

Irving's classic tale of the Catskill Mountain villager who falls asleep for twenty years, and then wakes up to find a changed world resembles in broad outline the Talmudic story of Choni the Circle Drawer who fell asleep for seventy years. Both men wake up to find a changed world.

Although there is no particular moral lesson that emerges from Rip Van Winkle's story, there are profound messages that emanate from the Choni tale. One message is that it is a good thing when a man performs good deeds, the consequences of which outlive him. The Talmud recounts the meeting between Choni and a man planting a carob tree that will not blossom for seventy years. When Choni questions the man about whether he will be alive to see the fruit of the tree, the man wisely informs Choni that his children will see the fruit and that is why he plants now. He is planting for future generations (Taanit 23a). Choni then falls asleep and, upon awakening, sees the practical outcome of that philosophy in his own life.

The second message is that people need to feel connected to others. That is part of being human. As an old man, Choni reveals who he is to the scholars of the day. They do not believe his story, and he dies feeling isolated from others. The Talmud forcefully derives from this narrative the adage, "either companionship or death (Taanit 23a)."

A teachable moment: Shirley Jackson's "The Lottery"

"The Lottery" indirectly examines the concept of *minhag*, custom, and how it influences present day behavior. The story begins in a matter-of-fact, ordinary way describing a rural community getting ready for a long anticipated communal lottery, which has been in existence for many years. Challenging this age-old ritual is out of the question. The lottery represents a connection to the past and to the town's sacred traditions, and cannot be tampered with. The narrative concludes with the revelation that the lottery "winner" will be stoned to death by the entire citizenry, raising the important issue of whether to preserve ancient customs when they are clearly destructive.

For me, the story provides an opportunity to discuss the Jewish concept of *minhag*, custom. A classroom exercise in comparing and contrasting "The Lottery" with the process by which customs in Judaism become part of Jewish life offers a way to show Judaism's enlightened approach towards the establishment of religious customs, one which is rooted in Torah sensibilities and life-affirming actions.

A teachable moment: Henry James' *Portrait of a Lady*

Henry James is a writer of nuances. Slight facial gestures or casual remarks convey a world of meaning. Body language can reveal secret thoughts. In one telling scene, Gilbert Osmond remains in his seat when Madame Merle enters, suggesting a familiarity with her that is unknown to others in the room. In truth, Osmond's failure to rise when she enters indicates a lack of respect for her as a woman. He has been intimate with her and his cavalier attitude to her is apparent to the careful observer.

The scene serves as a catalyst for a discussion of the importance of a physical gesture in communication. Jewish tradition tells us that even a slight grimace or frown can telegraph negative feelings about another person. Therefore, we have to be vigilant in scrutinizing our own behaviors, and not carelessly spread *lashon hara* (slander) about another human being through a facial expression any more than we should through words.

A teachable moment: Henry James' *Washington Square*

Sloper, Townsend, Penniman, Almond – these are the last names of characters in Henry James' novel. Names possess significance in literary works. Very often, they are clues to character. The name may indicate the character as he is now or as he will be in the future. Throughout the corpus of James' writings, names are used to suggest character, and this serves as a catalyst to discuss the significance of names in the Bible, and name changes that occur in the Bible.

For example, Jacob's name change from Jacob to Israel indicates a change in destiny. I relate this to the notion of changing the name of a seriously ill person in order to effect a change in that person's destiny. From a mystical perspective, if John Doe is destined to die and he changes his name to John Chaim Doe, his destiny can perhaps be altered. He is now not the same person he was, but a new creation with a new destiny.

A teachable moment: Alan Lightman's "In Computers"

Alan Lightman, poetically describing the power of the computer to reduce all of creation to mere storage data, highlights the power of the computer to remember everything. A powerful Mishna in the Ethics of the Fathers gives a similar message about God's observation of the world, cautioning men to behave properly since all our deeds are observed and recorded in the Heavenly Court.

Our Sages soberly remind us: "Everything is given on collateral, and a net is spread over all the living. The shop is open. The merchant extends credit. The ledger is open. The hand writes…. The collectors make their rounds constantly, every day, and collect payment from the person whether he realizes it or not. They have proof to rely upon. The judgment is a truthful judgment, and everything is prepared for the banquet (Avot 3:20)."

Furthermore, they tell us: "Reflect upon three things, and thou will not come within the power of sin. Know what is above you, a seeing Eye, and a hearing Ear, and all your deeds are written in a Book (Avot 2:1)." God does observe all our actions and does not forget anything, so that our ultimate destiny is determined based on the facts of how we lived. Nothing will be forgotten.

In the magnets of computers will
  be stored

Blend of sunset over wheat
  fields
Low thunder of gazelle.
Light, sweet wind on high
  ground
Vacuum stillness spreading from
  a thick snowfall.

Men will sit in rooms
upon the smooth, scrubbed earth
or stand in tunnels on the moon
and instruct themselves in how it
  was
Nothing will be lost.
Nothing will be lost.

A teachable moment: Henry Wadworth Longfellow's "The Arrow and the Song"

The power of song is to bring people together. After the splitting of the Red Sea, Miriam leads the women in song with a drum accompaniment. The sound of the drum resembles the sound of the heart; and when the people sing together, they express a unified communal heartbeat. Longfellow ruminates about the power of song in contrast to an arrow, a weapon of war. In the long run, it is the power of the human heart that survives and gives meaning to life. The ability of song to penetrate the heart becomes the climax of this brief but intellectually engaging verse.

I shot an arrow into the air,
It fell to earth, I knew not where;
For, so swiftly it flew, the sight
Could not follow it in its flight.

I breathed a song into the air,
It fell to earth, I knew not where;

For who has sight so keen and strong,
That it can follow the flight of song?

Long, long afterward, in an oak
I found the arrow, still unbroken;
And the song, from beginning to end,
I found again in the heart of a friend.

A teachable moment: Guy deMaupassant's "The Necklace" and D.H. Lawrence's "The Rocking Horse Winner"

Both of these stories deal with money, or rather the consequences of not having it. In "The Necklace," Mathilde borrows a necklace so she can appear to be a woman of stature at a social event. Her life spirals downward when she loses the necklace and devotes the rest of her life to paying for a replacement. Only after many years does she discover that the necklace that she borrowed was a worthless piece of glass, but it is too late for her to change things. She now lives with the consequences of her youthful obsession with material things.

In "The Rocking Horse Winner," a child is the story's center. He lives in a home where his mother constantly thinks about money and the lack of it. Her acquisitive nature is so ubiquitous that her son Paul feels that that the house is haunted, and he always hears the phrase "there must be more money" whispering to him through the walls of his house. Because he loves his mother and wants to alleviate her anxiety about money, he finds a way to predict the winners of horse races. As he rides his rocking horse with a violent yet hushed intensity, he goes into a kind of mystic trance and emerges with the knowledge of the winning horse. The story ends as Paul predicts the winner of a race that brings much wealth to his mother, but brings her tragedy as well when, moments after his prediction, Paul collapses and dies in his mother's arms.

I have used both these stories to discuss the Torah value of being content with what one possesses. As Ethics of the Fathers says: "Who is wealthy? He who is content with his lot." Both stories vividly describe the destructive nature of unbounded material desires.

A teachable moment: Herman Melville's *Moby Dick*

A reading of this classic American novel brings to mind a variety of symbols and themes, most notably through the white whale itself. Although white in color, it is black in destructive deeds. It is the focal point of Captain Ahab's quest and he pursues it with megalomaniac intensity.

Ahab is an angry man. Having lost his leg to the great white whale, he is bent on revenge and he will let nothing stand in his way. He rants: "Aye...it was that accursed white whale that razed me; made a poor pegging lubber of me ....I'll chase him round Good Hope, and round the Horn, and round the Norway Maelstrom, and round perdition's flames before I give him up. And this is what ye have shipped for, men! to chase that white whale on both sides of land, and over all sides of earth, till he spouts black blood and rolls fin out." It is this single-minded desire for revenge that ultimately is Ahab's undoing. His anger clouds his judgment.

Anger in the Jewish tradition is a major character flaw. It is associated with an inability to see things clearly and a propensity for making moral mistakes. As King Solomon reminds us in Proverbs, "A hot-tempered man commits many offenses (29:22)." The Talmud reinforces this idea in several places, and connects anger to arrogance. One who is angry foolishly thinks his view should prevail because he is right and others are wrong. He possesses a cockeyed sense of entitlement; he feels that everything should go his way. However, the Talmud cautions us against such thinking by relating the following: "Resh Lakish said- anyone who gets angry, if he is a sage, his wisdom leaves him; if he is a prophet, his prophecy leaves him (Pesachim 66b)." Furthermore, the Talmud states that an angry person is equated to an idolater: "He who rends his garments in anger, he who breaks his vessels in anger, and he who scatters money in anger, regard him as an idolater (Shabbat 105b)." In his desire to kill the whale, Ahab fails to see the human cost of his obsession. He loses his emotional balance and causes death to almost all the sailors on his ship. Ishmael is the lone survivor of the fatal confrontation between Ahab's crew and the whale.

Moby Dick is of interest not only for its theme of hubris and its tragic consequences, but also for its Biblical allusions. Ahab, of course, is the name of a Jewish king who did not have a share in the world to come because of his devotion to idol worship (Sanhedrin 90a). Rashi opines that, in fact, Ahab loved idolatry as much as a father loves his children (Sanhedrin 102b). The Biblical Ahab, like Melville's literary descendent, was single-minded in his rebellion against God, nature, and fate.

Another key figure in the novel is Ishmael, the only survivor of the Pequod's destruction. Ishmael is the name of the outcast, the exile, the man without a home; and the parallels to the Biblical Ishmael suggest a way to understand and interpret Ishmael's character. He is a man searching for a home, searching for security in an unpredictable world; and his journey could easily be ours.

A teachable moment: John Milton's "On His Blindness"

It is a Torah value to persevere in the face of adversity. In the grand scheme of things, God sometimes punishes us, but these afflictions are often referred to as "punishments of love." In some mysterious way, tribulations are vehicles of emotional and spiritual growth. This notion is expressed in Milton's poem "On His Blindness." Milton actually went blind at about age 46. Yet that affliction did not keep him from continuing to write and participate in life. It did not cause him to abandon his deep religious faith. He understood that God gives different trials to different men; and each man has to come to terms with his personal mission on earth, and how to deal with the circumstances in life that are beyond his control. Sometimes we serve God at center stage, and sometimes we serve him by standing in the wings.

When I consider how my light is spent
Ere half my days in this dark world and wide,
And that one talent which is death to hide
Lodged with me useless, though my soul more bent
To serve therewith my Maker, and present
My true account, lest He returning chide;
"Doth God exact day–labor, light denied?"
I fondly ask. But Patience, to prevent
That murmur, soon replies, "God doth not need
Either man's work or His own gifts. Who best
Bear His mild yoke, they serve his best. His best
Is kingly: Thousands at his bidding speed,
And post o'er land and ocean without rest;
They also serve who only stand and wait.

A teachable moment: Montaigne's *Essays*

The great French essayist, modest and humble in temperament, collected a large number of interesting insights that reflect Torah values. In fact, many of them directly echo aphorisms found in Ethics of the Fathers. Consider, for example, the following quotations of Montaigne: "...To judge a man, we must follow his traces long and carefully." "No wind works for the man who has no port or destination." "One courageous deed must not be taken to prove a man valiant." The overall observation is that man should be evaluated on the consistency of his character, not one event in his lifetime. This perspective is embedded in the statements of the Sages that we should judge the entire man favorably (Avot 1:6), and that we should not look at the container but at its contents (Avot 4:20). Do not be fooled by appearances.

A teachable moment: Frank Norris' *McTeague*

McTeague is a classic example of American naturalism. McTeague is a big, burly, uneducated man who works as a dentist on the frontier. Once he loses his job, he loses his sense of self-esteem as well. Moreover, his loss of job creates new tensions at home. His wife Trina, coming from modest means, now becomes fixated on money as an answer to her problems; and this sets the stage for continual bickering between McTeague and his wife.

Money becomes the central focus of Trina's life. In the privacy of her home, she speaks to herself, uttering her worship of money: "Ah, the dear money, the dear money.... I love you so! All mine every penny of it. No one shall ever, ever get you. How I've worked for you! How I've slaved and saved for you! And I'm going to get more; I'm going to get more, more, more; a little every day." Trina is driven to this state because of extreme circumstances; but nonetheless, her private words indicate that she has lost her social and spiritual moorings.

In class we discuss Trina's words; and, then, as a counterbalance, we discuss the Jewish response to wealth. Judaism does not frown on wealth, but our tradition tells us not to be too obsessive about possessions and money. In many places, our Rabbis remind us that the only thing we take from this world into the next is our good deeds. Therefore, it is wrong to make money and possessions the sole focus of our lives. The Ethics of the Fathers sums it up best: "Who is rich? He who is happy with his portion (Avot 4:1)." The key is balancing our needs with our wants.

A teachable moment: Plato's *Republic*

The World of Being and the World of Becoming define Plato's vision of human experience. There is a level of existence that relates to ideas, a world where everything is static. Juxtaposed against this static world is a world subject to change, a world that is mutable. This general concept in some measure is parallel to Judaism's notions of This World, *Olam Ha-zeh*, and the Next World, *Olam Ha-bah*. While the Platonic view of the world and god is not the same as the Torah notion of an all-powerful, personal God who involves himself in human history, it is useful to consider the similarities and differences between the Greek and Jewish perspectives on how we perceive the world around us. The similarities remind us that from time immemorial people, non-Jew and Jew, struggled to make sense of the universe, and the human quest for meaning knows no religious bounds. We share mankind's universal search for meaning, yet at the same time recognize that Jews have a specific pathway to follow.

A teachable moment: The Pearl Poet's "Sir Gawain and the Green Knight"

In teaching Arthurian material, it is natural to discuss the concept of courtly love, about which much is written. This story involves sexual temptation by a woman. The hero, Sir Gawain, is challenged to find a way to be responsive, courteous and kind to her, while at the same time preserving his moral code. This is a dilemma that resonates in a Jewish day school which encourages young men to postpone sexual gratification until marriage, and desires young men to be respectful and sensitive to women's feelings as well. Gawain must overcome temptation. The poet writes: "He feared for his name....But he feared even more what evil might follow his fall....*God help me*, thought the knight, *I can't let it happen!*" (Part 3, Chapter 26).

Two areas of fertile discussion can emerge from a discussion of this text. First is the manner in which young Jewish teenagers, boys and girls, learn to relate in a wholesome, respectful way to the opposite sex, and yet at the same time not be overly familiar in an indecent way. How do we relate to women generally becomes a discussion topic. How do we strike the right balance between normal, *halachically* healthy interaction and immodest behavior is the question.

A second discussion can revolve around the incident of Potiphar's temptation of Joseph. Are there similarities or differences? In both the story of Sir Gawain and the story of Joseph, it is morality that prevents the heroes from succumbing to temptation.

Other topics emerging from the narrative are hospitality to strangers and spiritual preparation before battle, two areas about which Judaism places great value.

A teachable moment: Edgar Allan Poe's "The Tell-Tale Heart"

Poe writes about men who test the limits of morality. His characters are motivated by revenge, by money, by fear. A classic tale is "The Tell-Tale Heart," which describes a gruesome murder of an old man, and the subsequent effort to cover up the crime. All goes well until the protagonist hears the constant beat of the dead man's heart. It is this deafening sound that eventually causes the murderer to confess.

I have used this story during the month of Elul in relationship to the topics of repentance and expiation of sin. Although the main character in Poe's story is perhaps a madman, the timely and relevant theme of confession/repentance runs through the story. It reminds us that when we commit a sin, there is a residue of it that remains with us far beyond the original crime. Moreover, we are challenged intellectually and emotionally to come to terms with our ethical lapses and mistakes. The story reminds us that we cannot escape ultimate responsibility for the terrible things we may do.

A teachable moment: Al Purdy's "Poem"

This touching poem by Al Purdy can describe the emotions of a parent towards a child or a child to an elderly parent. Or perhaps it simply describes a relationship between any two people who have a strong emotional connection, either familial or social. The speaker shares his feeling about caring for a sick loved one, knowing that this illness may be a foreshadowing of death. In this bleak setting, what counts most is being there for that other person.

This relates to the Jewish understanding of the mitzvah of *bikur cholim*, visiting and caring for the ill. The commandment to visit the sick is rooted in the general obligation of Jews to do *chesed*, to practice kindness, a *mitzvah* for which one receives reward not only in this world but the next, say our Sages (Shabbat 127a). Moreover, every morning in his prayers the Jew recites this passage from the Talmud to begin his Torah learning for the day. It is a *mitzvah* that is in the forefront of the minds of Jews from the moment they wake up. Furthermore, by visiting the sick, we emulate God who visited Abraham on the third day of recovery from circumcision. God is there not to talk to Abraham but just to be close to him. His presence alone alleviates the pain.

This is what is portrayed in Purdy's poem; namely, that being there for a sick person is what human beings should do for one another.

You are ill and so I lead you away
and put you to bed in the dark room
--you lie breathing softly and I hold your hand
feeling the fingertips relax as sleep comes

You will not sleep more than a few hours
and the illness is less serious than my anger or cruelty
and the dark bedroom is like a foretaste of other darknesses
to come later which all of us must endure alone
but here I am permitted to be with you

After a while in sleep your fingers clutch tightly
and I know that whatever may be happening
the fear coiled in dreams or the bright trespass of pain
there is nothing at all I can do except hold your hand
and not go away

A teachable moment: Sir Walter Raleigh's "What is Our Life?"

Jews at Rosh HaShanah (New Year) spend time in introspection, reflecting about the past year, making amends for one's mistakes, and resolving to do better in the coming year. Raleigh's poem sets up the context for a discussion about life's meaning in the shadow of oncoming mortality. Living in an age of spiritual belief, he notes that God is always watching us and this provides a catalyst for self-evaluation and ultimately self-improvement.

What is our life? A play of passion,
Our mirth the music of division
Our mothers' wombs the tiring-houses be,
Where we are dressed for this short comedy.
Heaven the judicious sharp spectator is,
That sits and marks still who doth act amiss.

Our graves that hide us from the searching sun
Are like drawn curtains when the play is done.
Thus march we, playing, to our latest rest,
Only we die in earnest, that's no jest.

A teachable moment: Edward Arlington Robinson's "Richard Cory"

The Ethics of the Fathers reminds us not to look at the container but at its contents (Avot 4:27). A Torah value is to see beneath the surface of things and to appreciate the importance of the inner life, a life not dependent on the acquisition of material things. This message emerges from the classic poem "Richard Cory."

Whenever Richard Cory went down town,
We people on the pavement looked at him:
He as a gentleman from sole to crown,
Clean-favoured and imperially slim.

And he as always quietly arrayed,
And he was always human when he talked;
But still he fluttered pulses when he said,
"Good morning!" and he glittered when he walked.

And he was rich, yes, richer than a king.
And admirably schooled in every grace:
In fine – we thought that he was everything
To make us wish that we were in his place.

Son on we worked and waited for the light,
And went without the meat and cursed the bread.
And Richard Cory, one calm summer night,
Went home and put a bullet in his head.

Appearances are deceiving and we should never judge a person by outward visage alone. Beneath the wealthy exterior may lurk an unhappy and tormented soul. We never truly know the inner life of another human being.

A teachable moment: Edmond Rostand's *Cyrano de Bergerac*

Cyrano de Bergerac, a nobleman in the French army, is a man of many talents, chief of which may be his ability to write love poetry. However, he possesses an extremely large nose, which deters him from making overtures to a beautiful woman. The plot of the play turns on his willingness to serve as the secret spokesman for a friend of his, who lacks poetical expression but who loves Roxanne, Cyrano's distant cousin.

Cyrano composes love poetry for Roxanne, but in the recesses of his heart he loves her too. He never openly confesses his love for her; but when he dies, Roxanne finally discovers the author of the love poetry directed to her.

Rostand's play evokes a fertile discussion of what is more important to a match, physical attraction or intellectual/emotional compatibility. The Ethics of the Fathers offers the maxim that one should not look at the container, that which is outward, but rather at the contents of the container, a person's inner qualities (Avot 4:27). Ultimately inward beauty, beauty of character, is what sustains a marriage. This sentiment is echoed in the *Eshet Chayil* (Woman of Valor) ode that is sung every Friday night by the Jewish husband as he serenades his wife with the words "grace is deceitful and beauty is vain; a God-fearing woman should be praised."

A teachable moment: William Shakespeare's *Hamlet*

Every father wants to give his son advice, wisdom that will enable him to navigate life successfully. A classic example of fatherly advice is Polonius' speech to his son. Laertes, in Act I, scene 3:

> Give every man thy ear, but few thy voice;
> Take every man's censure, but reserve thy judgment.
> Costly thy habit as thy purse can buy,
> But not express'd in fancy, not gaudy;
> For thy apparel oft proclaims the man....
> Neither a borrower nor a lender be;
> For loan oft loses both itself and friend,
> And borrowing dulls the edge of husbandry.
> This above all: to thine own self be true,
> And it must follow, as the night the day,
> Thou canst not then be false to any man.

In a similar vein, Rabbi Akiva offers fatherly wisdom to his son, Rabbi Yehoshua:

> My son, you should not sit and study in a conspicuous place in town (because many people will pass there and disturb your studies). You should not live in city where the municipal leaders are Torah scholars. (They will be busy studying and will not take care of the city's needs.) You should not enter your own house suddenly (without knocking on the door first), and you certainly should not barge into your neighbor's house unannounced. You should not go barefoot (for this is not becoming for a Torah scholar). Get up early in the morning and eat breakfast immediately....Treat your Shabbat like a weekday rather than be dependent on other people. And try to associate with a person on whom fortune is smiling (Pesachim 112a).

Another example of fatherly advice in the Talmud is Rabbi Mesharsia's counsel to his sons:

> When you go to your teacher (to attend his lecture), you should review the Mishna in advance (so that you are well prepared). And when you are sitting before your teacher, look at his face....And when you study your lesson, do it by the side of a stream; for just as the stream flows on, so may your learning continue on and on....(Keritot 6a).

Judaism is all about transmitting a legacy to the next generation. It begins with Abraham, Isaac, and Jacob and continues throughout the generations. Polonius' counsel to Laertes is a distant echo of a tradition that is rooted in the fabric of our oral transmission through the ages.

More teachable moments in William Shakespeare's *Hamlet*

Shakespeare's plays are rich with life wisdom. Many of the lines capture the essence of a Torah perspective of life. Moreover, some of his characters face challenges similar to those faced by Biblical heroes, and to contrast the Biblical with the Shakespearian protagonist is illuminating in both directions. For example, Hamlet feigns madness in order to hide his true intentions and confuse his adversaries. So too does David feign madness when he is fleeing from Saul and seeking refuge from his enemies. As Shakespeare writes "Though this be madness, yet there is method in't."

Moreover, in Hamlet's signature "To be or not to be" soliloquy, there are echoes of the adage from the Ethics of the Fathers that recommends us to consider the consequences of one's actions. Hamlet deliberates: "Whether 'tis nobler in the mind to suffer/ The slings and arrows of outrageous fortune/ Or to take arms against a sea of troubles/ And by opposing end them...." The Torah value of deliberating before taking action finds expression in these memorable lines of the great bard.

A teachable moment: William Shakespeare's "Sonnet 116"

The ode to the "woman of valor," the *Eshet Chayil* tribute to the Jewish woman, recited on every Friday night concludes with the statement that "Grace is deceitful and beauty is vain." It is a reminder to all Jewish men that what counts is inner beauty, which transcends the vicissitudes of time. This is the essential message of Shakespeare's sonnet. It is a love poem in which the speaker tells us that ultimate beauty is not just skin-deep. Shakespeare remarks, "Love is not love/ Which alters when it alteration finds." If our apprehension of love is only based on externals, then it will not last.

In class, I often ask my students why is it that old married couples seem to love one another more in their senior years than when they first got married. This question stimulates a discussion on the nature of love and how it grows over time when it is not solely connected to fleeting physical beauty. Shakespeare is interested in deep, lasting love, not transient affection.

Let me not to the marriage of true minds
Admit impediments. Love is not love
Which alters when it alteration finds,
Or bends with the remover to remove:
Oh, no! it is an ever-fixed mark,
That looks on tempests and is never shaken;
It is the star to every wandering bark,
Whose worth's unknown, although his height be taken.
Love's not Time's fool, though rosy lips and cheeks
Within his bending sickle's compass come;
Love alters not with his brief hours and weeks,
But bears it out even to the edge of doom.

If this be error and upon me proved,
I never writ, nor no man ever loved.

A teachable moment: Percy Bysshe Shelley's "Ozymandias"

King Solomon in Ecclesiastes says that all is vanity. The acquisition of material things does not bring man ultimate satisfaction or peace. The description of the great potentate's statue looking over a barren landscape expresses the Torah value of focusing on matters of the spirit rather than accumulating more and more possessions. The poem reminds us about leading a simple life rather than living a life devoted to amassing wealth.

I met a traveler from an antique land
Who said: 'Two vast and trunkless heads of stone
Stand in the desert. Near them, on the sand,
Half sunk, a shattered visage lies, whose frown,
And wrinkled lip, and sneer of cold command,
Tell that its sculptor well those passions read
Which yet survive, stamped on these lifeless things,
The hand that mocked them and the heart that fed.
And on the pedestal these words appear—
"My name is Ozymandias, king of kings:
Look on my works, ye Mighty, and despair!"
Nothing beside remains. Round the decay
Of that colossal wreck, boundless and bare
The lone and level sands stretch far away.

A teachable moment: John Steinbeck's "Flight"

"Flight" is the story of a young man's coming of age. The rite of passage, however, is not a formal religious ceremony. Rather, it is an act of violence. A young man cannot tolerate an insult and he murders the one who insulted him. As the protagonist Pepe says, "I am a man now, Mama. The man said names to me I could not allow." In a drunken argument, Pepe impulsively throws a knife and kills a man. The rest of the narrative describes Pepe's desperate flight to save himself from pursuers.

The story is a springboard for a discussion of all rites of passage into adulthood; but for me within the context of a Jewish day school, the conversation moves to a consideration of the meaning of Bar Mitzvah. The key operative word here is *mitzvah*. To be a "son" or "daughter" of the *mitzvah* (commandment) requires both physical and mental maturity. Once that happens, the child is responsible for one's behaviors. He is expected not to be impulsive, but rather to consider the consequences of his actions. The Ethics of the Fathers tells us: "A thirteen-year old becomes obliged to observe the commandments (Avot 5:25)." This in simple terms means that what God wants is more important than what we want. Accepting this notion is a sign of maturity.

A teachable moment: John Steinbeck's "The Pearl"

"The Pearl" is a simple story about a primitive people not used to wealth. When Kino, the main character, finds a pearl of great value, he thinks that it can bring salvation to his family and to his sick son, who has been bitten by a scorpion. As the story unfolds, possession of the pearl brings tragedy to Kino and his entire family.

The clear moral of the story, which reads as a folk tale, is that one should be content with one's lot. At the end of the narrative, Kino stares at the pearl, whose surface "was gray and ulcerous," and in the surface of the pearl he sees the face of a man he has killed and the face of his dead child. The pearl is now a malignant growth, not the harbinger of good tidings that he once thought it would be.

A discussion of this story leads to a consideration of the famous Mishna which tells us that a rich man is someone who is happy with what he has (Avot 4:1).

A teachable moment: Robert Louis Stevenson's *Dr. Jekyll and Mr. Hyde*

Stevenson's tale is about one man with two personalities, a natural jumping off point for a consideration of the good and evil inclinations within man. Stevenson suggests the difficulty of controlling negative impulses, especially after giving in frequently to one's sordid appetites. Therefore, one has to be vigilant always, for "sin is lying at the door (Genesis 4:7)." Man is challenged every day to make good choices and not give in to his base desires.

A teachable moment: Jonathan Swift's "A Modest Proposal"

In this classic satirical work, Swift proposes using young children for food in order to create a more favorable economic situation in Ireland. Essentially, the problem is that children are born to parents that cannot afford them; therefore, he proposes eating them. He observes that "a young healthy child well nursed is at a year old a most delicious, nourishing, and wholesome food, whether stewed, roasted, baked, or boiled; and I make no doubt that it will equally serve in a fricassee or a ragout."

I have used this satirical work as a trigger for a discussion of the Torah value of being fruitful and multiplying, of seeing children as an unmitigated blessing to parents.

A teachable moment: Amy Tan's "Two Kinds" and "Rules of the Game," two stories from *The Joy Luck Club*

"Two Kinds" tells the story of the immigrant experience and acute generation gap that occurs when parent and child are raised in two different cultures. The mother expects perfection while the child just wants to find herself in a strange and unfamiliar world. Tensions escalate when the mother gives the daughter piano lessons and the daughter does not fulfill the mother's musical expectations of her. After the death of her mother many years later, she revisits her parents' apartment and discovers her old piano recital books. As she plays the piano in a moment of nostalgia, she observes the titles of the two pieces in front of her on opposite pages: "Pleading Child" and "Perfectly Contented." She realizes they are two halves of the same song.

I use this story to parallel the Jewish immigrant experience and to show how it shaped the American Jewish experience. Only in retrospect can we see life in all its complexity. When we first live through an experience, we don't understand its implications. I share with the students the anecdote of the four sons in the Passover Hagadah. Some commentators see this as the progressive and inexorable deterioration of the generations when confronted with the challenges of modernity that characterized the Jewish immigrant experience in America in the early part of the twentieth century. Like the protagonist in "Two Kinds," American Jews can integrate the meaning of an experience into our lives and personalities only with the passage of time.

"Rules of the Game" also deals with the immigrant experience and the inherent generation gap that is part of it. Here, however, chess--not music--is the activity that becomes emblematic of the differences between the older and younger generations. The game of chess is first perceived by the mother as a waste of time. But, in the eyes of the child, Meimei, chess becomes the vehicle through which the child learns about life. She observes

> I learned why it is essential in the endgame to have foresight, a mathematical understanding of all possible moves, and patience; all weaknesses and advantages become evident to a strong adversary and are obscured to a tiring opponent. I discovered that for the whole game one must gather invisible strengths and see the endgame before the game begins.

This observation presents an opportunity for me to speak about the aphorism from the Talmud: "Who is a wise man? He who can anticipate the future (Tamid 32a)." It is a Torah value to consider the consequences of our acts. In that sense, the game of chess can serve as a metaphor for a Jewish approach to life, one that requires a person to think long and hard before acting.

A teachable moment: Alfred Lord Tennyson's "Ulysses"

It is a Jewish sensibility not to despair, to always pray for redemption and salvation, to hope for a better day. Rabbi Yochanan ben Zakkai epitomized this approach when he asked for the city of Yavneh from the Roman emperor Vespasian. Knowing the Temple was to be destroyed, he focused on the future. He knew that if Torah learning would survive, so would the Jewish people. In the Talmud Rabbi Akiva has a similar perspective on life when he observes foxes running over the Temple ruins. As painful as it is to see, he views this scene as the fulfillment of one dire prophecy of destruction that is a precursor to a brighter and happier prophecy in the future.

> Tho' much is taken, much abides; and though
> We are not now that strength which in old days
> Moved earth and heaven, that which we are, we are;
> One equal temper of heroic hearts,
> Made weak by time and fate, but strong in will
> To strive, to seek, to find, and not to yield.

In spite of destruction, in spite of adversity, the Torah approach is to persevere, knowing that God is orchestrating the redemption of the Jewish people from behind the scenes.

A teachable moment: Dylan Thomas' "Do Not Go Gentle Into That Good Night" and Ralph Waldo Emerson's "The Past"

Rabbi Yaakov tells us in the Ethics of the Fathers that one hour in this life is worth more than all the hours in the World to Come. The implicit reason is that in this world, we can still perform God's *mitzvoth* (commandments). In the next world, we simply experience the benefits of the life that we led here. After death, we can no longer change our eternal destiny. Thomas' poem can be used to illustrate man's desire to fight for life because it gives him the possibility for growth and achievement, for real action; hence, for meaning. In that sense, we do not want to die just as Moses did not want to die until he finished the task of bringing his people into the land of Israel. Life means that we still count. We are relevant. The Torah message here is to value each and every moment of life, even as we realize the inevitability of death.

> Do not go gentle into that good night,
> Old age should burn and rage at close of day;
> Rage, rage against the dying of the light.
>
> Though wise men at their end know dark is right,
> Because their words has forked no lightning they
> Do not go gentle into that good night.

Another message about aging emerges from a reading of Emerson's "The Past." Here the poet speaks of man's inability to change his destiny once he leaves this world. Therefore, we must use our time wisely in this world to prepare for the next.

> The debt is paid,
> The verdict said
> The Furies laid,

The plague is stayed,
All fortunes are made;
Turn the key and bolt the door,
Sweet is death forevermore.
Nor haughty hope, nor swart chagrin,
Nor murdering hate, can enter in.
All now is secure and fast;
Not the gods can shake the past;
Flies to the adamantine door
Bolted down forevermore.
None can re-enter there—
No thief so politic, No Satan with a royal trick
Steal in by window, chink, or hole,
To bind or unbind, add what lacked,
Insert a leaf, or forge a name,
New-face or finish what is packed,
Alter or mend eternal fact.

A teachable moment: Mark Twain's *Pudd'nhead Wilson*

On one level, *Pudd'nhead Wilson* is the story of David Wilson, an attorney whose hobby of fingerprinting babies enables him to ferret out the truth in a case of babies who are swapped at birth. His hobby is perceived by the townspeople as eccentric, and he is viewed as someone soft in the head; hence, a "pudd'nhead." On another level, it is a story about two children whose destinies are changed because one possesses wealth and the other does not. It is clear to the reader that wealth corrupts, and that leading a modest lifestyle is more conducive to the development of good character.

The Talmud expresses a similar message. The Sages tell us that "wealth gotten by vanity shall be diminished (Avodah Zarah 19a)." Furthermore, the Ethics of the Fathers tells us that true happiness comes to those who are happy with what they have (Avot 4:1). We see these Torah notions play out in the personalities of Tom Driscoll and Valet de Chambre. Tom is the son of a slave who is reared in a home of affluence, yet he gambles and drinks, revealing a predatory personality. Valet de Chambre, the son of a free white man who is reared in the home of slaves, develops into a young man of good character.

Another fascinating aspect of the novel is the way in which Pudd'nhead unravels the mystery of the babies switched at birth. Since he had come into town, he made a practice of fingerprinting all newborns, a hobby laughed at by most of his peers. But it is this hobby which eventually enables him to find out the truth. It is like the crucial DNA evidence in a television episode of "CSI," a program which revels in scientific data to solve crimes. Fingerprinting represents objective truth, and this is what Pudd'nhead stands for. It is this unwavering devotion to truth that is the core of his personality, and it is reflected in the age-old adage of the Ethics of the Fathers which states that one of the pillars upon which the world stands is truth (Avot 1:18). Pudd'nhead is synonymous with truth in the novel that bears his name.

A teachable moment: John Updike's "Perfection Wasted"

John Updike's poem speaks to the concept of individuality, the idea that everyone is unique and irreplaceable. A reading of the poem evokes a discussion of the notion of *tzelem elokim* (being created in the image of God). What precisely does that mean in literary terms and in spiritual terms? Many of the Sages interpret this to mean that just as God is unique, so too is each person unique. In the eyes of God, every human being is different from another, and from the aspect of eternity is irreplaceable. Updike deals with the idea in a casual, informal sense; but at its core, the poem affirms the uniqueness of every man.

And another regrettable thing about death
is the ceasing of your own brand of magic,
which took a whole life to develop and market—
the quips, the witticisms, the slant
adjusted to a few, those loved ones nearest
the lip of the stage, their soft faces blanched
in the footlight glow, their laughter close to tears,
their tears confused with their diamond earrings,
their warm pooled breath in and out with your heartbeat,
their response and your performance twinned.
The jokes over the phone. The memories packed
in the rapid-access file. The whole act.
Who will do it again? That's it: no one;
imitators and descendants aren't the same.

A teachable moment: Oscar Wilde's *The Picture of Dorian Gray*

The Picture of Dorian Gray, Oscar Wilde's only novel, describes the life of an exceptionally handsome young man who, in effect, makes a Faustian bargain to stay perpetually young while his portrait ages. Ultimately, his total devotion to a life of sensual gratification leaves him emotionally and morally bankrupt. Dorian takes to heart the philosophy of Lord Henry who tells him: "The only way to get rid of a temptation is to yield to it. Resist it, and your soul grows sick with longing for the things it has forbidden to itself...." Ironically, at the end of the narrative the same Lord Henry tells Dorian: "what does it profit a man if he gains the whole world and lose...his own soul?"

A reading of this novel about sensual gratification at the expense of moral sensibility brings to mind the character of Absalom, the son of King David who is focused on his own beauty and on satisfying his own lustful urges. The Talmud informs us that "Absalom gloried in his hair...and he cohabited with the ten concubines of his father (Soteh 9b)." Ultimately he met his death by being hung by his hair.

A comparison of Dorian Gray and Absalom illuminates the moral mistake of making a concern for outward appearances and sensual gratification the centerpieces of one's life.

A teachable moment: Tennessee William's plays

The central figures in his plays are all people who are seriously flawed. Consider *A Streetcar Named Desire*, *Cat on a Hot Tin Roof*, *Sweet Bird of Youth*, and *The Night of the Iguana*. The lead characters are complex and in some ways corrupt. But they are engaging characters who evoke audience empathy. I once asked my graduate school professor why Williams' protagonists were so appealing even though they embodied moral deficiency. In truth, the actors who played those parts were the iconic actors of the day, including such luminaries as Paul Newman, Richard Burton, and Marlon Brando. My professor quickly responded: "That's the point. Williams is telling us that immorality and moral turpitude can be seductive and attractive, and we have to be able to see beneath the surface when judging others." As Shakespeare says in *King Lear*, "The prince of darkness is a gentleman." We should never be fooled by appearances.

This notion figures in a discussion of the character of Laban, the duplicitous father-in-law of Jacob. His name in Hebrew mans "the white one." Conventional literary imagery relates white to virtue and black to evil. However, conventional imagery does not operate here. The Bible is reminding us with this name that we should not judge man by externals. As it so aptly states in the Ethics of the Fathers, "Do not look at the bottle but at what is inside of it (Avot 4:27)."

A teachable moment: William Wordsworth's "My Heart Leaps Up When I Behold"

It is a Torah sensibility to appreciate and value everything that God gives us. Nothing is to be taken for granted. We are to recognize the hand of God in everyday miracles, in the beauty of nature, in the stars at night, in the rising and setting sun. Wordsworth calls to mind a child's apprehension of the natural world and revels in its continual renewal and beauty. The poet encourages us never to lose the excitement of a child who sees things for the first time with a sense of awe. That is what the Psalmist would have us do when he reminds us that "God renews the world in his goodness each and every day."

> My heart leaps up when I behold
> A rainbow in the sky:
> So was it when my life began;
> So is it now I am a man;
> So be it when I shall grow old,
> Or let me die!
> The Child is father of the Man;
> And I could wish my days to be
> Bound each to each by natural piety.

A teachable moment: William Wordsworth's "Ode to Intimations of Immortality"

Jewish tradition time and time again encourages us to be positive, to see the glass as half full, to see things from the aspect of eternity and not to let the difficulties we face in life overwhelm us. Wordsworth's ode is a sobering, yet positive, reminder to see life as a process where we grow emotionally and intellectually and emerge from our challenges more savvy about ourselves and the universe. As we get older, our life choices narrow, but that does not have to mean that we lead lives devoid of meaning. Rather, maturity in life affords us the opportunity to see life as a journey, where the journey's final days are days of reconciliation with our more limited physical state and with our mortality. It is not a time for tears but a time for attaining wisdom. As the poet writes

Though nothing can bring back the hour
Of splendour in the grass, of glory in the flower;
We will grieve not, rather find
Strength in what remains behind;
In the primal sympathy
Which having been must ever be:
In the soothing thoughts that spring
Out of human suffering;
In the faith that looks through death,
In years that bring the philosophic mind.

A teachable moment: William Wordsworth's "It Is a Beauteous Evening, Calm and Free"

Wordsworth's poem captures the meditative mood of prayer at the end of the day. The value of prayer is great in Jewish tradition. Prayer is not just a recitation of words. It can also teach life lessons. There are three paradigms of prayer that are represented by the patriarchs, whose names are invoked at the beginning of the *Shemoneh Esrei*, the quintessential Jewish prayer. The patriarchs collectively taught the Jewish people how to pray and each had a different approach to communicating with God. Multiple patriarchs means multiple approaches. Each one reflects a different pathway, but leading to the same goal. Consider that the Bible stresses Abraham's early morning desire to serve God. Abraham is the early riser who seeks God at daybreak. Compare this to ee cummings' exuberant poem "I thank You God for most this amazing," where the poet sees the early morning as the time for man to celebrate his connection with the Almighty. In contrast, Isaac is depicted as seeing God in the late afternoon, for he is the spiritual founder of the afternoon service. His prayer is a meditation in a pleasant meadow, with the afternoon sun gently shining down upon the field where he is praying. This prefigures this scene of quiet holiness in Wordworth's "It is a Beauteous Evening Calm and Free."

It is a beauteous evening, calm and free,
The holy time is quiet as a Nun
Breathless with adoration; the broad sun
Is sinking down in its tranquility;
The gentleness of heaven broods o'er the Sea:
Listen! The mighty Being is awake,
And doth with his eternal motion make
A sound like thunder – everlastingly.

A teachable moment: William Wordsworth's "London, 1802"

Reverence for the elderly is a value in Judaism, particularly when the elderly are people of wisdom. Jewish tradition places the Torah scholar on a pedestal, for he is the one that can transmit to us instructions for living. The Torah scholar who is old can teach us wisdom because of his life's experiences and he can also help us make wise decisions if we counsel with him. In Wordsworth's poem, the speaker longs for the presence of the great poet and sage John Milton. If he were here, then London would be the better for it. So too it is with the Sages of old. If they were with us, the world would be a better place.

Milton! thou shouldst be living at this hour:
England hath need of thee: she is a fen
Of stagnant waters: altar, sword, and pen,
Fireside, the heroic wealth of hall and bower,
Have forfeited their ancient English dower
Of inward happiness. We are selfish men;
Oh! Raise us up, return to us again;
And give us manners, virtue, freedom, power.

A teachable moment: William Butler Yeats' "The Second Coming"

While this poem has a distinctly Christian context, the memorable lines in the first stanza describe a world devoid of spirituality and meaning, where brute force rules the day. I connect this to the Mishna in the Ethics of the Fathers that speaks of praying for the peace of the government, which, if lacking, results in a world of chaos and self-interest.

> Things fall apart; the centre cannot hold;
> Mere anarchy is loosed upon the world,
> The blood-dimmed tide is loosed, and everywhere
> The ceremony of innocence is drowned;
> The best lack all conviction, while the worst
> Are full of passionate intensity.

I also relate these words to the tumultuous time before the destruction of the Temples in Jerusalem, when Jews fought against each other and did not treat one another with respect. It was a time, say our Sages, when Jews observed the form but not the spirit of the law.

Film

aimonides tells us that we learn not only from God's words in the Torah but also from God's works, the natural world. The key is to develop the ability to discriminate between what is of value and what is mere dross in secular culture. The way to do this is to expose oneself to the great touchstones of literature and arts, while at same time being mindful of both the positive and potentially negative influences of such exposure. Culture can raise us up but it can also demean us if we are not thoughtful consumers.

With that in mind, I write about the cinema, the most ubiquitous twentieth century art form. The power of film to move us emotionally is immense, but too often contemporary film is vacuous and devoid of meaning. Given the reality that it is often difficult to find "kosher movies," films that have something valuable to say about the human condition, at the local cineplex, I choose to revisit what I think are worthwhile films from both the distant and recent past. The fact is that now moviegoing is a home experience as well as theatrical one. The Netflix phenomenon allows us to access great films of any time and place, both American and foreign, and to share them with friends and family.

In this section I share with the reader ten films which I recommend for their ability to give the viewer a broader and often wiser understanding of life, something which always animates the minds of thinking Jews. I have used these in informal settings with adults and with young people in my classroom as a teaching tool when dealing directly with cinema, and also when I felt that literary themes/works could be understood better if analyzed in cinematic terms.

I never show entire movies to a class, even in my film courses. While parts of films are certainly powerful examples of literary themes, it is rare that watching an entire film merits so much class time. Moreover, there are invariably scenes which may be inappropriate or objectionable to screen for a coed class of high school students. We live in a world where students do have access to such films; but within a school environment, I have chosen to show only specific scenes to highlight class discussions of particular motifs and topics.

The entire subject of the relationship between film and Judaic thought is vast and I hope to explore that topic in another volume. What I present here is only the beginning of a larger study.

Chariots of Fire (1981)

I first saw *Chariots of Fire*, a drama that had something to say about the nature of sports and the competitive drive, in 1981 when I myself was running five or six times a week. The film is about two men who are running in the 1924 Olympics: Eric Liddell, a young Scottish preacher, and Harold Abraham, a very competitive British Jew. The story chronicles their journey to Olympic glory, and in the process contrasts the lifestyles and worldviews of these two men.

A crux of the movie occurs when Liddell is asked to compete on Sunday, his Sabbath. He has to wrestle with his desire to compete and win on the one hand, and his desire to be faithful to his religious beliefs on the other. As the film unfolds, Liddell reveals a Jewish sensibility. He places principles before personal gain. Moreover, he understands that all his strength comes from God, and that all his earthly activities should express his connection with the divine.

In Jewish tradition, there is the notion that whatever we do in this world should be done to glorify God. Even mundane acts can acquire sanctity if we perform them with the right attitude. Eating can be a *mitzvah* if we eat to nourish our physical bodies in order to be strong to serve God. Sleeping can be a *mitzvah* if we sleep in order to give our bodies needed rest so that we can rise like a lion on the morrow to do God's work. It is this mindset that exemplifies the character of Eric Liddell. He sees life as an opportunity to serve his Creator, and he sees his achievements as emanating not just from his own efforts but also from God's personal involvement in his destiny.

The Ethics of the Fathers tells us that we can and should learn from every man, both Jew and non-Jew. In *Chariots of Fire*, Eric Liddell reminds us to place spiritual integrity over worldly glory.

A Cry in the Dark (1988)

The power of slander is the topic of this 1988 film starring Meryl Streep as Lindy Chamberlain. The movie is based on a true story of an Australian murder trial of a mother accused of killing her daughter. The body is never found, but a bias against a woman who is seen as cold and unfeeling by her peers creates a mob hysteria that destroys her reputation and unravels her emotionally. Our tradition tells us that every person is presumed to possess a *chezkat kashrut* (a presumption of being an upright individual) unless proven otherwise. The Torah commands us in many places not to be a talebearer, not to embarrass someone, to always give someone the benefit of the doubt. Yet this is difficult to do when the object of our comments is someone whom we dislike. The fact is, however, that this is precisely the time when we have to overcome our instincts to judge someone unfairly. This is the time when we have to withhold judgment until we have all the facts.

The destructive effects of prejudice are grippingly dramatized in a pivotal scene in the movie. Lindy, exhausted from the trauma of losing a daughter and then being suspected of murdering her, is giving testimony in a courtroom in a cold, dispassionate way; and the jurors see her as an insensitive mother who might, indeed, have murdered her own child. As the prosecutor relentlessly cross-examines her, the interrogation is intercut with scenes of ordinary people in the street commenting on her guilt, offering interpretations of why she did it, and feeding the publicity frenzy. As one watches the montage of images, one gets a real sense of the emotional pain Lindy is suffering when giving evidence of her dead child's death by a dingo, a wild dog, before a mistrusting audience of jurors and lay people who have come to watch the spectacle with detached amusement.

A Cry in the Dark on a literal level refers to the cry of a baby in the night. On a thematic level, it refers to the cry for compassion and understanding in a world that is often insensitive to the emotional pain of other people, where the public desire to know trumps sensitivity to other human beings.

Searching for Bobby Fischer (1993)

As an undergraduate student at Yeshiva University many years ago, I had the opportunity to watch Bobby Fischer play chess. I do not know how to play chess, but a friend of mine who did was participating in a school-wide competition between the students and the chess master, who would play all of them simultaneously. I still remember coming down to the school cafeteria and watching nearly a hundred young men set up their chess boards on long tables preparing for their match with Bobby who would stroll down the various aisles making his moves quickly as his opponents reflected on what to do next. To my knowledge, no student won his match that night; but it was fascinating to observe this chess genius casually dispose of so many opponents in so short a time.

Searching for Bobby Fischer is a film about chess; but, more importantly, it is a film about life. We watch as little Josh Waitzkin develops a love of chess. He is fascinated by the game and enjoys watching the exciting contests of speed chess in Washington Square Park in New York City. His mother senses his love of the game and pays to have him play one of the players in the park. His interest in the game grows, and his father decides to get him a top flight teacher. Josh studies with the guru but still retains his childlike interests and attitude. Basically, Josh is the kind of person who wants to be nice to other people. He does not hate his opponents, nor does he look at them as objects to destroy. His mother, on listening to Josh's wish to help a friend, tells him "You have a good heart. That's the most important thing in the world."

It is this conflict between being nice and being a winner that is the subtext for this sports film about chess. As Josh achieves success in tournaments, his father becomes possessed with his son's genius at playing the game. Frank Waitzkin comes to see chess not as game nor as science, but rather as pure art. The notion that his son plays like Bobby Fischer animates his ego and he begins to push Josh harder. He, more than Josh, wants the glory, the attention, the honor that he never received in his life. Frank pursues the ephemeral goal of fame, and forgets about balance in life. As Josh advances in skills, his teacher Bruce puts him through exercises designed to toughen Josh mentally. But Josh is a boy who likes and respects other people. His coach's desire to make him like Bobby Fischer "who held the world in contempt" evokes a simple, direct response from Josh; "I'm not him." His mother sharpens that observation when she tells her husband that "Josh is not weak. He's decent."

Several Torah themes are embedded in *Searching for Bobby Fischer.* In Proverbs, there is the wise directive to "train the child in the way that he goes (Proverbs 22:6)." The message here is that parents need to understand the uniqueness of their children. Different children possess different personalities, different interests, and different proclivities. That is the lesson that Frank Waitzkin learns as he first pushes Josh to excel, and then comes to recognize Josh for the decent boy that he was and is. Frank ultimately realizes that the game of chess does not define his son, who is much more than a chess player. He is a good son, a caring friend, and a decent human being who wants balance in life.

We also learn from the film that wisdom can come from many places, from parents, from a speed chess hustler in Washington Park, and from a serious teacher of chess. Notably, all are present for Josh's crucial match at the Chess Grand National Tournament in Chicago, the site of the film's finale. Our Sages in the Ethics of the Fathers explicitly tell us: "Who is wise? He who learns from every man (Avot 4:1)." Everyone has something to teach us if we are a careful observer of mankind.

Finally, we learn that the pursuit of fame is illusive. The more one runs after it, the more difficult it is to acquire. Finally, fame in the Jewish view is acquired through the simple acts of friendship and kindness that punctuate our lives. The film ends with Josh putting his arm over the shoulder of a friend who has just lost a match and telling him, "You're a much stronger player than I was at your age." As the credits begin to roll, a coda informs us that "while Josh still plays chess, he also plays baseball, basketball, football and soccer, and in the summer, goes fishing." Josh intuitively understands that a fulfilling and meaningful life is a life with balance.

The Road Home (1999)

The title of the film *The Road Home*, a beautifully rendered Chinese movie directed by Zhang Yimou, alludes to the journey of a man to his final resting place. Specifically it refers to the tradition of carrying the coffin to the grave so that the deceased "doesn't lose his way." This is a movie about deeply held traditions that both animate and connect people over the span of many generations, traditions that link them to the past and to the future.

The film opens as an urban man is returning to the rural village of his birth to bury his father, a revered teacher who brought wisdom to many generations of youngsters in his primitive schoolhouse. Looking at the photo of his parents, the movie launches into an extended flashback of the courtship of his father and mother many years ago. It is a romance based not so much on physical attraction, although there is that element, but mostly on a shared understanding of life and a common destiny.

After this poetically charged story of courtship, the film returns to the preparations for the funeral, which will require a long half-day march to the burial site in the midst of a blinding snow storm. Everybody in the village wants to participate in this tradition of escorting the dead, especially when it is a way to show respect for a beloved teacher. Their affection for him is palpable as we watch the villagers vie for the opportunity to carry the bier despite the inclement weather.

As a final mark of respect and tribute for his father, the son, on the day after the funeral, teaches a lesson in the village schoolhouse which is about to be demolished. He stands before the children, echoing the instruction of his father. The subtitles emblazoned on the bottom of the screen reveal clearly the life lessons imparted by his father: "In everything there is a purpose. Know the past. Know respect for your elders." By encouraging the students to appreciate and value the past, he assures them of a meaningful present and future. The teacher is the glue that binds the generations.

Torah values are ubiquitous in the movie. There is the value of respect for elders, the value of respect for tradition, the value of honoring the dead by escorting them to the burial site, the value of a loving relationship founded on common values and not just physical attraction, and the value of finding meaning in adversity. Ecclesiastes tells us that "it is better to visit a house of mourning than a house of feasting, for that is the end of all men and the living will lay it to his heart (7:2)." In the case of *The Road Home*, the loss of a loved one becomes the road to greater self-understanding.

Castaway (2000)

The opening scenes of *Castaway* set the stage for a meditation on time. A FedEx pickup rolls into a rural Texas farm and picks up a package that is destined for Moscow. We follow the package as it journeys to Russia in the dead of winter. In Moscow, Chuck Noland, a company exec is lecturing Russian workers in the Russian FedEx facility about the need for timely delivery. He shouts: "We live or die by the clock." He tells them that losing time is a sin, and he berates them for not being more conscientious.

On his return flight to Russia, he overhears that his friend's wife has cancer and her future is uncertain. The camera focuses on Chuck's face as he contemplates for a brief moment the precariousness of life. The scene then switches to Memphis at Christmas time, where Chuck has been courting Kelly, his girlfriend, for several years. Marriage is on his mind, but he rushes to leave because of a work obligation. As he says goodbye to Kelly at the airport, they exchange gifts. She gives him a family heirloom, a locket/timepiece with a photo of her inside; he gives her a box with an engagement ring, saying that he will officially give it to her on New Year's Day when he returns. Ironically, his last words to her are "I'll be right back."

What happens next takes up the bulk of the film's plot. Chuck's plane crashes, he is marooned on a remote island for four years during which time he struggles for survival. At home in Memphis, Kelly, thinking that Chuck is dead, has married and had a child. Life has moved on.

The narrative arc of the movie brings us back at the end to Texas where Chuck, played by Tom Hanks, delivers a package that was on the plane the day of the fateful crash. After he delivers it, he returns to a desolate country crossroads, the proverbial fork in the road; and the film closes with Chuck looking out at the various roads he can choose. He is now a wiser man contemplating which direction to take, considering how to make the most out of life and the time he has left.

A fundamental Jewish idea is embedded in this film: the value of time. The Ethics of the Fathers strongly remind us that we should not delay doing worthwhile tasks. "If not now, then when (Avot 1:14)," say our Sages. We should not drift through life but rather make the most of the time God allots to us.

Moreover, Rashi, the celebrated medieval Torah scholar, quoting a Talmudic passage (Pesachim 48b) urges us to take advantage of every mitzvah opportunity that comes our way. He compares the words *matza* (unleavened bread) and *mitzvah* (commandment) and derives that both are intrinsically connected to time. The *matza* must be prepared in a timely way, and so too should we perform *mitzvot* in a timely way, immediately, and not postpone doing a good deed. *Castaway* reminds us of the fleeting nature of time, implicitly encouraging us not to delay life's important and most satisfying obligations.

Shattered Glass (2003)

Shattered Glass is a story ostensibly about journalism and its commitment to truthful reportage. An early scene in the film depicts Stephen Glass, a successful journalist, sharing his wisdom with an avid group of high school students who may aspire to be writers one day. Glass's presentation is warm, infectious, and devoid of egotism. He writes for *The New Republic*, the "in-flight magazine of Air Force One," and tells his young fans that when you write for such an influential magazine, "your work gets read by people that matter." Surely this is a heady job, but he cautions the students that reporters have to be responsible for what they write and there is more to the job than simply getting your name into print. Journalism ultimately is about the pursuit of truth, and that is what makes it important.

All this is a preamble for an account of deception and lies. As the movie unfolds, we see Stephen fabricating story after story in a working environment where fact-checking is critical. Because he is an entertaining presence at staff meetings, he ingratiates himself with his fellow employees, who are unsuspecting of his lack of ethics. When an Internet magazine uncovers the deception, Stephen's imaginary world falls apart. He has spun a web of lies from which he cannot extricate himself, and he begins blaming others instead of accepting responsibility for his actions.

Shattered Glass is a powerful morality lesson depicting what transpires when we lack integrity, when there is no respect for truth. The Ethics of the Fathers tells us that one of the pillars upon which the world stands is truth (Avot 1:18). Without that essential element, societies cannot exist. The film also presents the consequences of losing a good name: loss of job, loss of credibility. Our Sages remind us that one's good name is the most important possession we have. Rabbi Shimon says: "There are three crowns—the crown of Torah, the crown of priesthood, and the crown of kingship, but the crown of a good name surpasses them all (Avot 4:17)." Furthermore, we see how the pursuit of fame is ephemeral. The more one pursues it, the more it eludes him. Countless statements in the Talmud reinforce this notion: "He who seeks fame loses his reputation (Avot 1:13);" "A desire for honor removes a man from the world (Avot 4:28);" "Do not desire honor (Avot 6:5)."

Finally, *Shattered Glass* provides an example of the adage in the Ethics of the Fathers that tells us "Whoever desecrates the Name of Heaven in secret, they will exact punishment from him in public (Avot 4:5)." Stephen Glass is a liar, a distorter of truth in order to promote his own image. In the end, his deception is revealed in a public way, not only in the news media but in the film that is cleverly titled *Shattered Glass*.

Bella (2006)

"One moment can change your life forever" is the advertising tagline for *Bella*, and it proves to be true in the case of Jose, a star soccer player, who on the day of his contract signing experiences a life-changing moment. Near the beginning of the film, one of the characters says, "If you want to make God laugh, tell Him your plans." This adage of an old grandmother highlights one of the essential messages of the movie; namely, that we are not in full control of our destinies, and it is foolish to think that we are. Jose has planned a life as a soccer icon, but the uncertainties of life lead him to a different destiny.

Jose works as the head chef in a restaurant owed by his adopted brother. He is a master chef; but when he sees his brother treat Nina, a waitress, callously, he leaves the kitchen to console her after she has been summarily fired. Soon he discovers that Nina is pregnant, and morning sickness has caused her lateness to work. As Jose and Nina walk the streets of New York together, they meet a blind street vendor with a sign behind his stand which reads: "God closed my eyes. Now I can see." This sets the stage for each of the main characters to undergo a spiritual transformation, which brings with it a new understanding of life, its adversities, and its possibilities.

The street sign with its message of hope provides the spiritual subtext of *Bella*. Jose and Nina both have experienced hard times; yet Jose, especially, tries to use his tragic past to build a hopeful future for himself and Nina. Jose is a man of faith who comes from a family of faith. They say grace before eating and are mindful of the presence of God in their lives. They celebrate life together and are joyful in their relationships with friends. Their wisdom and energy are infectious, and Nina basks in their warm presence.

Through a day's quiet conversation between Jose and Nina, Nina overcomes her aversion towards carrying her baby to term, and decides to accept motherhood. To Jose, this represents an affirmation of life. Jose is a person who values people, who values life, and his goal is to affirm life in any way that he can. He not only encourages Nina to have her child, but he also, in a different context, reprimands his brother when he treats his employees cavalierly. He berates his brother for only being concerned about business, and not caring enough about the people who work for him. "It's all about you," he shouts when he wants his brother to think about his workers.

After a long day and night of conversation with Nina outside of the city, they return the next morning. As the camera follows them, the soundtrack plays a spiritual song which emphasizes the soulful state of the protagonists at this point. Some of the words are the following: "O Lord, I have heard Your voice...I am closer to Thee....by the power of grace divine, let my soul look up with a steadfast hope, my will be lost in Thine."

There is much to admire in *Bella*. A central theme is repentance. How do we atone for a grave sin? How can we get forgiveness from someone who is no longer alive? Do we have to atone for a sin that we committed inadvertently? All these questions are discussed in the codes of Jewish law, and the dilemmas that Jose faces can be viewed in the classic context of Jewish repentance literature. Moreover, the film demonstrates the value of family as a positive force to help one overcome challenges in life. A loving and supportive family is critical to Jose's ability to cope with personal tragedy. Other people might choose illicit drugs to escape a painful reality, but Jose is not part of that culture.

Above all, *Bella* presents not only a story of personal tragedy and redemption, but also a story of one act of kindness that is transformational in the life of another person, Nina. The Ethics of the Fathers reinforces the importance of kindness when it tells us that it is one of the three pillars upon which the world is based (Avot 1:2). Kindness is an eternal attribute of the Jewish people, and this seminal life lesson of kindness is embedded in the gentle and thoughtful narrative of *Bella*.

Stranger than Fiction (2006)

Harold Crick is an IRS agent whose life is defined by numbers. He also is a lonely man with few friends. The film opens with the viewer observing Harold's robotic lifestyle, where everything is calculated down to the last second. Then the camera switches to brief scenes of a little boy receiving the gift of a bicycle from his parents and an African-American woman looking for a job. These two characters appear at various points in the movie, and one wonders why since they seemingly have no connection to the plot.

Harold begins to hear a writer's voice narrating what is happening to him at that moment. He is aware of the voice, but cannot fathom how it can describe his every action as he experiences it. The conceit of the film is that an author, Karen Eiffel, is actually writing his life, leaving him with little free will to exercise. It is a frightening when Harold realizes the reality that he no longer is in control of his destiny, especially when Karen writes that he will die "imminently." The circuitous plot of the film describes Harold's attempt to come to terms with his seeming inability to affect his future.

This realization that life will end soon moves Harold to be more proactive in the life he has left. He begins a romantic relationship and even learns to play the guitar. Our Jewish tradition tells us that we do not know the day of our death; it could be any day. For example, our Sages teach us to "repent one day before your death (Avot 2:15)." The commentators explain this to mean that since no man knows the day of his death, he should repent every day. In other words, make every day a special day and fill it with meaning. We should value time and value the people with whom we come into contact.

Harold understands this life lesson. One of his mentors in the film poetically observes that only we can determine if our life will be a comedy or a tragedy. Will our lives affirm the continuity of life or the inevitability of death? The believing Jew lives with this constant dialectic as he makes decisions each and every day of his life.

The lives of the boy on the bike, the black woman who is a bus driver and Harold finally converge in the last segment of the film. Harold is at a bus stop and the boy on the bicycle rides in front of the bus. Harold reaches out to save the boy and is hit by the bus. Does he die as the author writes or does he live and exercise free will? The film raises the question of how much free will does man have. Jewish tradition tells us that God is in charge of the world, but God gives man a limited area to exercise free will. As our Sages write in the Ethics of the Fathers, "everything is foreseen, yet freedom of choice is given....everything depends on the abundance of good deeds (Avot 3:19)."

Man's destiny is not totally pre-determined. Man cannot change some things, but there are some things he can do, and that is what *Stranger than Fiction* affirms. In the face of an all- knowing Author, God, man can still influence his destiny, especially through the performance of a good deed, which is what Harold does when he saves the boy who rides in front of the bus.

Moreover, the film presents a morally sensitive character in the author, Karen Eiffel. She decides to change the tragic ending of her novel. She changes it from a literary perspective; she moves it from a masterpiece to just an okay work of fiction in order to protect and save someone. What is paramount to her in the final analysis is not fame but doing the right thing. Morality trumps personal ego.

The movie concludes with Eiffel reminding the viewer/reader that we need to thank God for the small pleasures of life that we often take for granted in our busy daily lives, for the "accessories of life" that are here to serve nobler causes and save our lives emotionally and spiritually. She speaks of the importance of the loving gesture, the subtle encouragement, the warm embrace. It is these little things that make life precious. Harold Crick appreciates this truth when he finds life after almost losing it.

The Visitor (2007)

The Visitor is the story of Walter Vale, a disillusioned college professor who has recently lost his beloved wife of many years. Since her death, he has become even more reclusive than before and solitude is his preferred state. However, his quiet and predictable world unravels when two illegal immigrants, a white male from Syria and a black woman from Senegal, mistakenly take up residence in his Manhattan apartment. At first he wants them to leave, but recognizing their vulnerability in being sent out at night to find new lodgings, he invites them to stay. Their sojourn in his apartment lasts many days during which deep friendship grows between him and his tenants.

Walter develops an interest in hand drumming, which is recognized by his tenant Tarek, a Syrian immigrant who is an accomplished drummer. Tarek teaches Walter some techniques which enable him to play the djembe reasonably well. This interest in drumming captivates Walter, indirectly propelling him towards more human connections. He plays with a drum circle in Central Park and shares the rhythms with people of varied cultures. The drum represents a kind of communal heartbeat which links all men, and Walter breaks out of his aloneness to join the family of mankind.

The story takes a tragic turn when Tarek is picked up by the police and placed in a Queens detention center. Tarek's mother comes from Michigan to visit her son in New York since she has not heard from him in a while. When she discovers that he is incarcerated and may be deported, Walter intervenes and hires an immigration lawyer to help. In spite of his best efforts, Tarek is deported, motivating his mother to leave the States to go to Syria to be with her son. Although Tarek is likely to have a grim future, Walter has been transformed by his friendship with Tarek, Zainab, and Tarek's mother. He has moved from being a solitary man to a man who wants to connect with other people. The last scene of the film depicts Walter in an underground subway station playing the djembe, making a very loud drum sound, which metaphorically expresses Walter's new heartfelt approach to life.

Our Sages tell us "not to separate from the community (Avot 2:5)." It is spiritually dangerous to be alone. Solitude can lead to depression and an unhealthy preoccupation with oneself. Therefore, it is good to be involved with others and to feel the distress of others; for one who feels another's pain shares it with him and, in a sense, lessens the emotional burden of the sufferer. Walter's attempt to help another makes him a better man, a man who is alive to himself and to others. Moreover, the Torah tells us in many places to take care of the stranger, the one who is most defenseless in society, for we were once strangers in Egypt as well. This empathy for the outsider is a hallmark of a Torah personality; and Walter, a very decent man, becomes an even better man when he understands the plight of the stranger and does something to alleviate the stranger's problem. By helping others, he helps himself.

The Diving Bell and the Butterfly (2007)

The Diving Bell and the Butterfly is one of the most unusual and powerful films that I have ever seen. On the surface, it is about Jean-Dominique Bauby, a French fashion magazine editor, who suffers a stroke, which leaves him unable to speak or to move his body. He is suffering "locked-in syndrome," a rare malady which only allows him to communicate by blinking his left eye.

What is unusual about the film is that the viewer sees the world from the point of view of Jean-Dominique. The entire first half-hour depicts his realization of his paralyzed state and his initial efforts to communicate to those around him.

All of us have seen handicapped people, but the inner struggle that goes on inside the mind of the handicapped is largely unknown to us. We can sympathize, but we cannot really understand the overwhelming emotional darkness and isolation of one who lives daily with physical challenges. Now, through this film, we get a glimmer of understanding about life lived with physical limitations.

In this sense, the movie is an instructive teaching tool. It compels the viewer, through its forceful and naturalistic imagery, to be thankful each day for being ambulatory, for possessing the ability to speak and to communicate freely with others.

When a dear friend of mine would be asked how he was doing, he always responded, "*Baruch Hashem*, thank God, fantastic." He did this because he truly felt thankful for the everyday miracles with which he was blessed. Watching *The Diving Bell and the Butterfly* will make you appreciate life more. Do the math and count your blessings.

Credits

W.H. Auden. "Musee des Beaux Arts," copyright 1940 and renewed 1968, from *W.H. Auden: Collected Poems*. Random House.

W.H. Auden. "The Unknown Citizen," copyright 1940 and renewed 1968, from *W.H. Auden: Collected Poems*. Random House.

Countee Cullen. "Any Human to Another" from *On These I Stand*. Copyright held by the Amistad Research Center, Administered by Thompson and Thompson.

e.e. cummings. "I thank You God for most this amazing" from *Complete Poems: 1904-1962*. Liveright.

e.e. cummings. "next to of course god America I" from *Complete Poems: 1904-1962*. Liveright.

Henry Dumas. "Thought" from *Poetry for My People*. Eugene Redmond and Loretta Dumas.

Robert Frost. "The Road Not Taken" from *The Poetry of Robert Frost*. Henry Holt and Company.

Robert Frost. "Mending Walls" from *The Poetry of Robert Frost*. Henry Holt & Company.

Robert Frost. "Stopping by Woods on a Snowy Evening" from *The Poetry of Robert Frost*. Henry Holt & Company.

Robert Hayden. "Those Winter Sundays" from *Collected Poems of Robert Hayden*. Liveright.

Shirley Jackson. "The Lottery" from *The Lottery* by Shirley Jackson. Farrar, Straus & Giroux.

C. Day Lewis. "Song" from *The Complete Poems*. Sinclair-Stevenson.

Alan P. Lightman. "In Computers." First appeared in *Science 82*.

Arthur Miller. *The Crucible*. Penguin.

Al Purdy. "Poem" from *"Beyond Remembering*: *The Collected Poems of Al Purdy,* edited by Sam Solecki, Harbour Publishing, 2000.

Theodore Roethke. "Snake" from *The Collected Poems of Theodore Roethke*. Doubleday.

John Steinbeck. "Flight" from *The Long Valley*. Penguin.

Amy Tan. "The Rules of the Game" from *The Joy Luck Club*. Penguin.

Amy Tan. "Two Kinds" from *The Joy Luck Club*. Penguin.

Dylan Thomas. "Do Not Go Gentle Into That Good Night" from *Poems of Dylan Thomas*. New Directions.

John Updike. "Perfection Wasted" from *Collected Poems 1953-1993*. Alfred A. Knopf, a division of Random House.

About the Author

Rabbi Herbert J. Cohen, a veteran educator for over thirty years, has taught both Judaic and secular classes throughout his career. Possessing a PhD in English as well as rabbinic ordination, he enjoys the discovery of common threads in religious and secular studies, which illuminate each other and give the reader new understandings of both Torah and secular literature.

Rabbi Cohen presently lives in Dallas, Texas, where he is Family Educator with the Community Kollel of Dallas, an adult institute of Jewish learning. He has written four books including *The One of Us: A Life in Jewish Education*; *Kosher Parenting: A Guide for Raising Kids in a Complex World*; *Torah from Texas: Perspectives on the Weekly Torah Portion*, as well as *Walking in Two Worlds: Visioning Torah Concepts through Secular Studies*.

Rabbi Cohen can be reached at rabbihjco@msn.com.

Cover art by Meryl Cohen

The Torah is called a tree of life. "Sacred Forest" represents Torah in its variegated forms as it is revealed both in the sacred and secular worlds.